MARTINI

A memoir

FRANK
MOORHOUSE

KNOPF

'. . . it was an employment for his idle time, which

was then not idly spent.'

Izaak Walton, *The Compleat Angler* (1653)

A Knopf book
Published by Random House Australia Pty Ltd
20 Alfred Street, Milsons Point, NSW 2061
http://www.randomhouse.com.au

Sydney   New York   Toronto
London   Auckland   Johannesburg

First published in 2005

National Library of Australia
Cataloguing-in-Publication Entry

Moorhouse, Frank, 1938–.
Martini: a memoir.

ISBN 1 74051 312 6.

1. Moorhouse, Frank, 1938–. 2. Martinis. 3. Cocktails.
I. Title.

641.874

Cover image courtesy of Getty Images
Cover and internal design by Greendot Design
Typeset in 11/16 Filosofia by Midland Typesetters, Australia
Printed and bound by Griffin Press, Netley, South Australia

10 9 8 7 6 5 4 3 2 1

I dedicate this book to my dear friend and agent for

many years, Rosemary Creswell, who guided and aided

me in many aspects of my life and writing.

CONTENTS

Martini

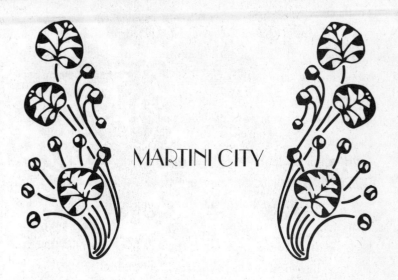

MARTINI CITY

My friend V. I. Voltz, the Manhattan identity, and I had our first martini made from Plymouth gin in Cambridge, England, in Browns, under the revolving fans, amid the ferns and cane chairs. I was writer-in-residence at King's College and he was working on 'a project', although I am led to believe he is a man of independent means. The Plymouth gin martini to which I had just introduced him is made from that gin that has a four-master sailing ship on its label. The label says, 'Navy strength'.

Martinis are made from either London gin or Plymouth gin (which confusingly is technically a 'London gin') and no others (there is something called Old Tom gin – a sweet gin which has just about disappeared from bars, so we won't worry about that, sorry Old Tom) and never from Dutch gin or sloe gin (made from the small bluish-black sloe fruit with a sharp, sour taste, sometimes called Blackthorn Plum) which are both drinks that go their own ways.

Martini in one hand, the other hand in his overcoat pocket, Voltz watched the bartenders. 'They don't care. Deliberation is one of the ingredients of the martini,' he said. 'It has to be made with deliberation. To care about the martini shows that you know what it is that goes to make that which could be called, in life, *fine*.'

After a moment of thoughtful silence, Voltz said, 'All that's *truly* fine.' And then, 'All that's truly fine *in life*.'

I could tell that Voltz, standing there in his long, black Clintonesque overcoat, was not at ease in Browns. Truth be told, he is never at ease far from West Greenwich Village, although he claims to have a special affection for St Petersburg. To ward off criticism of my choice of cocktail bar, I said, 'I'm afraid this is the only bar in Cambridge that serves a martini with any confidence.'

'Confidence, as we know, in anything, is never enough,' Voltz said. 'The bartender should be able to talk a little about the drink he has crafted, discuss your preferences. Should acknowledge that you are a martini drinker, not just any off-the-street drinker. In life, there are drinkers and there are martini drinkers.'

'In art, sincerity is never enough,' I said.

'Nor enthusiasm,' Voltz added. 'And nor are sincerity and enthusiasm in combination.'

'Nor diligence.'

'Not sincerity, enthusiasm, diligence or confidence in sum total.'

There was too much light in Browns bar, albeit English light. 'A martini bar has to be dim – never sunny,' I said, feeling that

I had to assert my own connoisseurship. 'The company, too, is an ingredient of the martini.'

'Alone is good,' Voltz said.

'Alone is fine. Without the stress of human company.'

We sat down.

'There are martini cities,' Voltz offered when uncomfortably sat, legs stretched out, still in his overcoat. 'And there are cities in which you should never order a martini – I am increasingly unsure of Cambridge, England.'

I had never thought about a 'martini city'. It was another Voltz insight. 'You are right, Voltz, there are martini cities.'

'Las Vegas was once a martini city,' he said. 'It might have been a martini city in the 1950s, but it isn't any longer. Lake Tahoe, perhaps, on a fall day.'

I had never been to Lake Tahoe on a fall day but the way Voltz said it made me want to be at Lake Tahoe on a fall day, drinking a martini with him.

'A martini city has a lustre of which only martini drinkers are aware,' Voltz said, returning to the idea, swirling his martini, eating the olive and putting the pip in his overcoat pocket. 'Such a city must be in Europe or the New World. Most of all it has to have the merit of being connected to books or movies or to the history of the martini. I would include some parts of Central Europe.'

'I think Dunedin, New Zealand, is a martini city,' I said, playing a wild card. 'It is the furthest southern point of civilisation, a sombre, seaside university city of some culture. A poet, James K. Baxter, who was once banned came from there. James K. Baxter was New Zealand's Ginsberg. Or vice versa.

When I was there having a nervous breakdown three years ago, I had a martini made by a thoughtful bartender who knew of James K. Baxter and took good care of me.' As I spoke, I felt a slight panic that I would not be able to successfully defend my nomination of Dunedin as a martini city.

'I wouldn't know about Dunedin, New Zealand,' Voltz said, pulling a face as he drank, presumably again tasting the Plymouth gin martini which I now feared was also a mistake. 'I know nothing about Dunedin, New Zealand. Or James K. Baxter. No disrespect. In my eyes, that you once had a nervous breakdown there is sufficient merit and I so proclaim it.'

'Thank you for that compliment. I am not arguing for Dunedin with strong conviction. I wanted to demonstrate that you cannot always be certain whether a city is going to qualify as a martini city or not at first glance. The only line of Baxter's I remember is "A man's body is a meeting house".'

'Be that as it may about a man's body,' Voltz said, 'New Delhi, for example, is definitely not a martini city.'

Oh, I had heard differently but I could see that Dunedin might be more of a candidate than New Delhi – *on first glance*. 'New Delhi, no, not on first glance, although I have heard people talk highly of martinis from New Delhi.'

'I seriously doubt that New Delhi could be a martini city,' Voltz said. 'Regardless of what these people you know say. It is culturally too far from the source. A drink to have in the city of New Delhi might be the G and T or maybe a Chota Peg.'

'Curiously, Tehran would be a contender,' I said, flirting for his favour by offering yet another seemingly implausible city.

4

Voltz looked at me, knowing that I knew something about Tehran that he did not. His ploy was to show no curiosity, banking, I suppose, on my not being able to keep silent about my little Tehran secret for too long.

Perhaps with India in mind, for our second martini we went back to Bombay Sapphire gin with its ten botanicals (a 'London' gin regardless of the name, having no connection with Bombay). Voltz said he found the Plymouth gin 'prickly' and likened it to having a nettle placed on one's tongue. I said that I myself did not mind an assertive gin because I chose to believe that they were the gins drunk in Gin Alley and in Hogarth's drawings.

'Cities aside, do you know the perfect bar for drinking a martini?' Voltz asked. Drinking with Voltz could become something of a life test.

My mind wandered around the bars of the world and came to settle on the Bayswater Brasserie in Sydney, but before I could come up with a more exotic answer, Voltz said, 'A bar car on a train. The bar car on a train in Central Europe or North America, travelling first class.'

Perfect. Sometimes Voltz, with his identification of the exquisite in human experience, is at times a magician. Of course a bar car on a train was the perfect martini bar, overlaid as it was with echoes of many great movies and novels, and with its suggestion of detachment from worldly concern, and with the undefined promise contained within all great journeys.

'Probably on a train before World War II,' I added.

Voltz looked at me and considered this and then nodded at my refinement and he sipped his martini with a face that showed the lament that comes from sensing that we are in the wrong place, and perhaps living at the wrong time in history, and as a consequence, but also as a compensation, we are therefore remote from the self-important busyness around us and from all the clamouring news of the world and all its endeavours, events and claims.

I added another refinement. 'Watching the landscape receding rather than approaching.'

He thought about this and nodded, saying, 'You're right about that too: receding not approaching.'

'There is a nice paradox in the bar of a train being the perfect martini bar: it is in no city; it is disengaged from dwellings and from landscape. It is an imperturbable space.'

Voltz nodded again. 'That's right, an imperturbable space.' I could tell he was savouring the phrase. 'Another of the great paradoxes of the martini.'

'As a matter of interest, Voltz, have you ever drunk a martini on a plane?'

'Never.'

'Nor I. Not even in first class. It is unimaginable.'

'They have nowhere to properly chill everything down. And furthermore, the martini glass should always be served filled to the brim. That's not possible on a plane.'

I asked Voltz what the filling of the glass to the brim was all about.

'It's a salute,' he said.

'To what?'

'A salute to your guest. It says "no half measures", or at least, "today there will be no half measures". It represents the spirit of generosity and full-heartedness. Amplitude.'

'Is that where the term "no half measure" comes from?'

'I suspect so,' said Voltz. 'I suspect much of our wisdom comes from the martini. Directly or indirectly, that is.'

'That may be going too far.'

'I don't think so.'

I told Voltz that I had been doing some work on the two-martinis-only rule, something we had considered many times over the years. I said that I'd discovered that the hazards of the third drink goes back a long way. That the 17th Century English poet George Herbert had written, 'Drink not the third glass, which thou canst not tame when once it is within thee.'

'It's good that they knew about the third drink in the 17th Century. They probably disregarded it as frequently as we do. That's why they had to bring in the rule.'

'Sometimes it is said that the first drink is for amiability, the second for a silver tongue, and the third for a heart of gold.'

'I enjoy scholarship,' Voltz said.

I said to Voltz that my publisher, Jane Palfreyman, once said to me that sometimes the edge of the night had to be jumped over. She said that three martinis was the cape to lay over the puddle of the night. Four was the pole to vault over the night altogether and land on another planet.

Voltz lit up. 'I think I like this Jane Palfreyman, your publisher.'

I continued, 'As you know only too well, I myself argue for the third drink and for all the good and unexpected things it may bring. Including the fourth drink. Another old saying is that the third drink is for temptation, the fourth is for folly.'

'As well as scholarship you seem to be full of old sayings.'

'It comes from being at King's College,' I said.

'Temptation,' Voltz said, 'I consider to be an enlivened state of being and that happy folly always sorts itself out. That's what I've discovered in life. You must put all this in your lecture on the martini you have in Shanghai and other dark cities.'

'I will. You think I should become known as "someone who lectures on the martini"?'

'Worse things could happen to a person.'

'Suppose so.'

'Between the wars they drank martinis in the Black Cat in Shanghai – Baker in Paris said the martini was invented at the Black Cat in 1928 by Baron Clappique and André Malraux.'

Voltz and I looked at each other with the expression that said, 'Yeah, right'.

Voltz then reminded me that the famous Dorothy Parker martini poem combines folly and temptation in one stanza. We quoted it together.

> 'l like to have a martini
> Two at the very most
> After three I'm under the table
> After four I'm under my host.'

'Did you know that Dorothy Parker died alone complaining that she was broke but there were hundreds of uncashed cheques found in the drawers of her apartment?'

'I didn't know that,' he said.

We drank our toast to Dorothy and ordered our third martini without discussion or hesitation.

THE STORY

I first wrote about the martini cocktail when I was in my thirties, well before I met Voltz. It was a story entitled 'Martini', which is in the book *Forty-Seventeen*.

The story tells of an older man with his much younger lover at a beach house early in their affair.

The man is teaching the girl how to make a martini.

Martini

He mixed the martini in the jug, stirring with studied performance. 'Always stirred never shaken,' he told her.

'I've never drunk a martini in my life.' She made it sound as if she were now fifty and had astoundingly missed the martini. Instead, she was seventeen and with no reason to have tasted a martini. 'We can pretend we are in New York.'

'Paris. It was actually invented by a Frenchman. And it's named after an Italian.'

'All right. If you like you can be in Paris and I'll be in New York. I really want to be in New York.'

'That'd be no fun.'

'We could call each other from those nightclub table telephones.'

'I like to know the vermouth is there in the martini,' he said, in a donnish way, sniffing the jug for the vermouth. 'Many don't. The great martini drinkers just want the gin mixed with mystique. Let a beam of light pass through the vermouth bottle and strike the gin – that was sufficient, saith Luis Bunuel.'

'Who is Luis Bunuel again? I know you told me once.'

'Bunuel is a Spanish film director. When we are in Spain we'll go –'

She broke in, '*Belle de Jour*? Right?'

'Correct. I took you to see it in some town in Victoria.'

'What I remember is you in the motel afterwards.' She giggled.

'When we go to Spain we'll go to Bunuel's birthplace.'

'You made me take money from you.'

'Aragon.'

'You showed me how a whore does it. And why do we have to go to people's birthplaces?'

He hadn't answered that question before. 'You are too questioning. You go to the birthplaces of people you admire to see where the magic started. You go to see if you can be touched by the magic. To see if there is any left.'

He poured the martinis and carefully carried the brimful glasses to her on the balcony of the beach house.

'You're incredible,' she said, taking her martini, 'you've even brought along the proper glasses. I know they're martini glasses, that much I do know.'

'The glass is half the drink.'

'As you always say.'

Was he beginning to repeat himself?

He looked out at the sea in which he'd swum as a boy. 'I've never made love to anyone here in my home town – you are the first. That's unbelievable in a way, given that I lived here until I was seventeen, your age –'

She broke in again. 'I'm eighteen now – you keep forgetting, you want me to stay seventeen, you find it sexy.'

'Sorry. But it took me to now, well getting towards forty, to have sex in the place where I was born. Says something.' He tried to muse on this but nothing occurred to him.

'What does it say?'

'I don't know yet.'

'Was it different? Our sex?'

He kissed her fingers, one still slightly pen-callused from her schooling. 'It's always different with you.'

'No slimy answers,' she said. 'Tell me how it was different, I want to know.'

'*Did thee feel the earth move?*'

'Don't make fun of me. *For Whom the Bell Tolls*?' She said the name of the book as she would give an answer in a classroom.

'Different for me because it connected with "formative circuits",' he teased. 'Do you want me to say things like that? Or poetry?'

'Whatever screwing circuits. Tell me.'

'I think you seek poetry.' He couldn't tell her now. 'I'll tell you when I've found the words. I'll write you a sonnet.'

'Do you know "The Schooling of Sex"?'

He looked at her and shook his head.

'"Below the waist is at first geography, and then it becomes maths, and then it becomes poetry, and then it becomes current affairs, and then it's history."' She giggled, and rushed to say, 'I know that's a bit infantile. It's what we used to say at high school.'

That is, last year. 'I don't get the geography bit.'

'Oh – as a kid, below the waist was referred to as "down there" or "below the belt" – like "below the equator", I suppose there are boundaries there too, and unknown country. It's just kids' stuff.'

He grinned. Her youthfulness was a delight to him far greater than she could understand. Was his age intriguing to her?

'The maths is from the way boys score sex – 2-4-6-8-10 – 2 is upstairs outside etc.'

'Yes, I remember all that.'

As for their sex together, it was different because he was getting emotional cross-tunings, like a radio with a crowded dial.

'Another thing,' he said, 'is that it's my parents' home. Or at least their beach house. Which will do.'

'Will do what?'

She bridled when she sensed he was using the conversation to talk to himself.

'There is always, you know, *the mother*, always the mother, but even if the bed we're using is not the bed where I was conceived, it's close enough.'

'Yuck.' She moved swiftly away from that, saying, 'It's a beautiful drink. I could become really hooked on martinis. But what do you do with the olive, do you eat it at the beginning or at the end of the drink or is it just a . . . garnish?'

Garnish, nice word.

'That's a personal preference. It's useful to play with during the conversation. You can prick it with the toothpick and the olive oil seeps out.' He did it. 'See, the olive oil comes into the drink.'

She looked at the drink and then said, 'The olive on the toothpick gives the drink an axis.'

He looked back to the martini and its glass and the toothpick. She was so right.

She pricked her olive.

Regardless of the cross-tunings he was getting, seeking, he wanted also to imprint at the very same time, a uniqueness onto their experience. To mark her off from his crowded personal history. He had used up so many of his markers of distinctiveness, had *been there* in so many intimate situations – although it never ceased to surprise him that every relationship seemed to throw up its own distinction, regardless of any superficial similarity. Sexuality did seem to be infinite in its variations. But she couldn't be his *first*, well, first anything just about, not his first love, first wife, nor first adultery, not even his first seventeen-year-old, his ex-wife had been that – and he couldn't give to her any of the body's six or seven significant virginities, although at seventeen – eighteen – she herself seemed to have exhausted most of her own already. Well, not all. And one, perhaps two, he wasn't sure, she'd given to him, but not the primary virginity. And they did share also some sensual firsts of the minor scale. He supposed he was trying to consecrate their experience by bringing her to his home territory, into the aura of kin, if not kin. He wanted to rank her equal with love if not *as love*. He couldn't tell her this yet. As future *wife*? Probably not feasible.

She spoke, breaking his thoughts. 'The olive is like leaking radioactivity,' she said. She was preoccupied with nuclear war but not so much as a political issue – more as a macabre fireworks, as human inclination to self-destruction or as a video game.

'I'll give you a twist of lemon next,' he said, 'that's the other classic garnish.'

She moved herself against him, began to arouse him with her hand, but he was in another mood and said, 'I thought this was the cocktail hour.'

'I want to get rid of that sad look.'

'I'm not sad.'

But cross-tunings were coming in across the sea from his youthful marriage to a girl from his home town (although they'd never had sex in their home town – except for some vaguely recalled, fumbled caressing on a river rock in bushland, a 'full dressed rehearsal' which he chose not to count). And a surprising, unmentioned, almost involuntary ejaculation in a classroom late one afternoon – no joining of their bodies.

The cross-tunings were entries of ill-handled love, their artless fumbled living back then.

Momentarily, his mind left their cocktail hour, going back to a cocktail hour years before.

❀

In the sedate lounge of the Windsor, he called the waiter. 'This martini is not cold enough, we asked for it very cold, and very dry. It is neither.'

He was relieved that at twenty he had got the complaint out, slowly, and with some authority.

'Yes, sir.' The waiter went to take their drinks away.

'Leave mine,' Margaret said. 'Mine's all right.' She put her hand out over the drink.

The waiter took away his glass.

'You are a pain in the arse sometimes,' his wife said.

'Waiter!' He turned back to her. 'I thought you were big on consumer rights.'

The waiter came back to the table. 'Take my wife's martini also – we'll both have a fresh one, cold, very cold.'

'Yes, sir.'

She let the waiter take the drink this time.

'You give me the shits,' she said. 'So much for a second wedding anniversary.'

He said nothing.

'Fighting with waiters is not my idea of a good time. The drink was alcohol, isn't that what you care about?'

He knew that he'd complained to the waiter as a way

of getting at her. He didn't really care about the coldness.

He wanted to be in New York drinking martinis in Costello's bar with Thurber in the thirties. With the sophisticated Louise. He bet that Louise had been to Costello's bar. He'd get there one day soon. 'I wish I was in New York. In Costello's, only Americans know how to mix a martini.'

'What would you know about Costello's? Or New York?'

'Travel isn't the only way of knowing a place.'

'Anyhow, the martini was invented by a Frenchman,' she said with a superior tone.

'Crap.'

'Have it your own way.'

'Where did you hear that crap?'

'I read it in *The Origin of Everything*.'

'Crap.'

'And stop big-noting yourself,' she went on. 'You're just a country boy – you've drunk only one martini before in your whole life. You get it all from Scott Fitzgerald.'

He remained silent, stung. Then he turned in on himself and began relishing a secret score against her – that two days before they'd left for their anniversary trip he'd drunk martinis in bed with Louise, his first 'older woman'.

Perversely, while relishing this private memory, he reached across to take her hand, gaining himself virtue for making the move to heal their domestic friction while at the same time betraying her in his reverie.

'I'm sorry,' she said, joining in the reconciliation, taking the blame onto herself.

'We don't have to stay the country boy and the country girl all our lives.'

She held onto his hand. 'I'm quite happy to be the country girl,' she said, quietly.

※

'Stirred, never shaken,' Louise said, putting a finger on the tip of his nose to emphasise her point, stopping him with her other hand.

He'd been doing an American bartender act with the cocktail shaker, Louise being the first person he'd known to own a cocktail shaker.

'That's how I've seen it done in American movies.'

Louise laughed. 'You have been going to the wrong movies, darling. There are some cocktails we do that way, my love, but not the martini, never the martini.'

'That's how we do them in my home town,' he said, trying to joke over his naivety.

'I believe that.'

He put the shaker down and removed the top and looked into it. 'They seem all right, they haven't exploded.'

'They'll be bruised,' she laughed, 'or at least that's what an aficionado would say.'

'Should I throw them away and start again?'

'No – I'm sure we can drink them with impunity – and I have an idea.'

He stopped himself from asking who the aficionados were.

He began to pour them but Louise again stopped him. 'Tch, tch,' taking away the wine glasses he'd taken out and bringing back martini glasses. 'A classic drink demands a classic glass. And my idea is that we take the martinis to the bedroom and watch the sun set over the city. And fill them to the brim.'

She led him to her bedroom, he slightly trembling with desire, the martini slightly spilling. He watched as she changed into a clinging, silk nightdress. She was the only woman he had known to wear a real nightdress.

Looking out on the city at dusk from her bed he felt regret that he should be doing this against his young wife, felt the abrasion of his spirit. But it was numbed away with the lust for Louise, Louise who had the skills of living and such seeming completeness of life.

'What's wrong, love – guilt?' Louise asked.

'No,' he lied.

'What's the matter?'

He turned over in bed to face the question from his seventeen-year-old – eighteen-year-old – girlfriend.

'Memories spooking about,' he said. Her word.

'But you said you hadn't brought anyone else here.'

'That's true,' he said, putting a hand to her face, in awe of her youth, 'but the heart is a hotel.'

He reached over and took his martini from beside the bed and finished it.

Where had his young wife learned about the origins of the martini back then? He had looked in the book *The Origins of Everything*, she hadn't got it from there. He would love it to be that she'd learned it from an older lover at the same time he'd been unfaithful. He'd love that to be the case. It would equalise the guilt. But more, it would be fantastic symmetry. But it was too fanciful.

'I don't want you thinking of other women while you are sexing on with me.'

He smiled. 'They have their rights.'

She rolled on to him, straddled him, and began to arouse him again. 'No they don't,' she said, 'all other lovers are banished.'

'Mix another drink,' he said, 'first.' Louise had instructed him never to say 'another' drink.

She left the bed and went into the bar, her naked, youthful grace tightened his heart. He called to her. 'Should never say "*another* drink".'

He saw her look into the cocktail jug. 'There's some left,' she said.

'It'll be mainly melted ice.'

He was taking from her the flavours of young, first love. He guessed she was engaged in her own private explorations.

'I'll make a new lot, tell me how, again,' she called.

He was collecting pleasures not taken when he'd been seventeen because of gaucheness. He was taking also perhaps the last taste he'd ever have of pure youth.

The first martini, though, had honoured, he felt, his ex-wife and Louise. This one would be theirs.

'One part vermouth, five parts gin,' he called back to her. 'Some would argue – but that's my mix now.'

THE PAGEANT OF LEARNING

The story is fictionally autobiographical in the sense that it somewhat rearranges time and people from my life while telling something about my life.

In a sense, I was the young man who was taught the martini by an older woman lover – a beautiful and sophisticated woman named Norma Crinion, now dead, and back then quite older than myself; and I was the embarrassing young husband – around twenty – who was so gauche with his young wife in the hotel lounge. It never took place in the Windsor. And whatever my ex-wife and I argued about it wasn't the martini. But the sort of argument we had was like that. As for sexual relationships with another generation, they can be especially significant, intimate doorways to the world of another generation and also a return to one's own earlier age, at least on a flying visit. I told my writing students at Texas last year that every writer should have two cross-generational relationships – one when young, one when older.

In my life the first infidelity was not with Norma but with a man, Paul J, ten years older than I, who became my lover when I was a teenager, although I had seduced him. I had not 'relished' the infidelity except in moments of sexual ecstasy. At the time, I suffered dreadfully from the panic of it, until it became part of my life.

Norma actually came later after my marriage had ended when I was about twenty-three. But it was Norma who taught me about the martini and other ways of the world. I told Norma about my sexual predilections – it was not a surprise to her, nor was it anything she had not encountered before – and it was she who took me to my first tranny nightclub, The Purple Onion. I was recently told that the expression purple onion is gay slang for the engorged head of the penis. Of course.

To return to the story. I was the older man who taught his girl-lover about martinis, I was the older man who ultimately had his heart very seriously broken by this girl but that is another story – some of it told in *Forty-Seventeen*.

I see that in the story, the martini in some ways represents worldliness and also perhaps the elixir of life, the magic potion. At the University of Texas, I realised while reading student stories related to drug experiences, that drugs are also seen as a magic potion. The history of the magic potion stretches back in fiction and folklore, potions that change us into animals, give us wisdom, give us beauty, give us sexual prowess, give us access to special places and experiences: make us invisible, Faust, Alice in Wonderland – 'drink me, eat me'. In a way, I guess my martini story observes and celebrates one of the pageants of learning, the metaphorical passing on of wisdom through sexual intimacy, sometimes a graceful and wonderful thing, sometimes not so graceful. Nor painless.

EMAIL TO OPHELIA IN NEW YORK

'. . . I am working on some engrossing and agonising projects and yes, the *Martini memoir* is one of them – musings on whether I have spent the richest of lives or the most wretched of lives – but the book unfolds a chapter or two of *Forty-Seventeen* (mainly the chapter 'Martini') into their own stories or Stories Not Told from that book. Perhaps the book will be about a man who becomes lost in his memoirs and his stories and who can no longer make shape of his own life, only of his stories.

'Or is it about how a writer becomes lost and bewildered within his own stories while writing his memoir? Lost forever wandering in his stories.

'You and your delicious book *The Favourite: Sarah, Duchess of Marlborough*, the Sarah who would have preferred her breast to be a manly one, were discussed at a lunch at the Hornes last week. See, Ophelia, you are talked about. It would be fascinating to be able to have a snapshot of all the places and circumstances in which we were referred to in our absence, say, in the last week, everywhere in the world: at committees, in the dreams of others, in consideration by higher authorities for awards, prizes, medals, at meals in restaurants and homes, by cleaning staff in hotels, in bed by former lovers recounting their connections with us to their new lovers, by family members, by enemies who have met us and by enemies who have never met us, by strangers who have heard rumours and stories about us, readers who have come across our work, people we have taught, people who have taught us, who have heard our public talks, and in the fantasies of would-be lovers. By Death and his committee . . . By Disease and her committee. We could advertise in likely newspapers and magazines asking people who had mentioned our names on a certain date to contact us . . . mmmm, no, wouldn't work.

'Perhaps my book is about vestiges, and the use of vestiges, meaning a trace or piece of evidence; a sign, as in vestiges of an earlier civilisation; found no vestige of their presence; a particle; without a vestige of clothing; showed not a vestige of decency; or in biology where it means a part or organ of an organism that is reduced or functionless but was well developed in its ancestors. I see that the word comes from the Latin word *vestigium*, meaning "footprint".

'Or perhaps also figments, meaning things invented or existing only in the imagination from the Latin *fingere*, "to fashion".'

Ophelia is a writer and a policy analyst for Human Rights' Watch in New York and the daughter of London-based journalist Michele Field. I lived with them both for a time, years ago. Ophelia was ten when I tried to teach her to ride a bike. I didn't succeed.

Michele introduced me to the use of 3×5 note cards as a system and to the pocket wallet to hold them — the most important organisational innovation and tool-for-thinking-and-writing I have in my life. I think that as a writing system it is as important to me as the laptop computer.

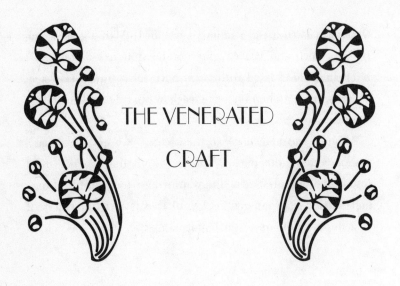

THE VENERATED CRAFT

The martini tradition is perhaps the most elaborate and most elegant of all the drinking games — a sophisticated way of playing the fool. For what seems such a simple drink the martini is a whole lumbering wagontrain of rules and traditions and all martini drinkers fancy themselves as the Wagon Masters, the Keepers of the Lore — take Voltz as an example. Folklorists classify their material beginning with the general category *Food and Drink* then down to particulars, so to *drink* (N) and then to *alcoholic beverage* (N 447), then to *distilled*, N447.4 and then on and on. The martini makes its way into many categories: *belief, riddle, proverb, craft, ritual, ceremony, festival, game, tale, custom, transformation, special vessel,* maybe *sacrament*, and more.

Traditionally from the 19th Century, the martini is a drink of gin with dry vermouth added in proportions according to taste. From the 1920s increasingly the amount of vermouth added decreased dramatically, although Roger Angell in an essay on the martini in the *New Yorker* says he has a sister-in-law who likes what he calls an upside-down martini – a martini with the usual proportions reversed: that is, a drink which is mostly vermouth with a little gin.

The classic martini is served icy cold with an unpitted green olive on a wooden toothpick in a conical glass on a stem (Voltz has much to say about the size of the glass; he thinks the glasses used today for the martini are far too large).

The first primary variation of the classic is the addition of more olives – sometimes up to three.

The second variation is the use of a twist of lemon instead of the olive.

The third acceptable variation is the use of a twist of lime instead of the lemon.

The fourth acceptable variation is the use of vodka instead of gin.

The secondary variations are pretty near infinite.

There is a cocktail misleadingly called The Perfect Martini where sweet vermouth is used instead of dry, a drink which I have never seen ordered although it has interesting historical links to the fast crowd in Europe in the 1920s.

The word martini now seems to have slipped into a wider meaning and is sometimes used to describe any concocted cocktail served in a martini glass; other drinks have appropriated the martini glass and Voltz and I are not happy about it.

In the 'Martini' story the man tells his young lover that his mix is now 'one part vermouth, five parts gin'. I like that mix, but I find that I also intuitively vary it a little either way – sometimes dryer, sometimes not. I have become flexible. That may be a worry. Voltz never varies his – one part vermouth, six parts gin.

Thousands of cocktail-hour stories surround the martini, usually about the Right Way to make it.

In another story from my book *Forty-Seventeen* the older man tells his young lover the story of the Martini Rescue – what to do when lost in the forest.

'"You do not panic. You do not walk aimlessly. You find a shady spot with a fine view, you sit down, you take out the cocktail shaker, the gin, the vermouth, and the olives from your back pack (which every sophisticated trekker carries) and mix yourself a martini. If there is a glacier nearby you chip off some ice to chill everything down.

'"You will not be lost for long. Within a few minutes someone will come from nowhere, tap your arm and say, excuse me, you are not doing that right – that is not the way to make a proper martini."'

I came across another version of this martini joke from World War II in Roger Angell's *New Yorker* essay. Navy pilots were given a survival kit to be opened only if they were forced to ditch their plane. The kit contained a tiny shaker, a miniature martini glass, a thimbleful of gin, an eyedropper of vermouth. The pilots were told that in the event of a crash they were to open the kit and mix themselves a martini.

Within a minute a rescue boat would appear and the captain would shout out through his megaphone, 'That is not the right way to make a dry martini.'

Apart from agreement on the shape of the glass – if not size of the glass – the rules and practices for every other part of the martini process are argued about and tinkered with.

I was going to say that the only other thing agreed upon about the making of a martini is that the martini must be cold, very cold. The gin can be kept in the household freezer compartment because it is not possible to freeze a bottle of gin in a household freezer compartment. But I recall an amendment to the coldness rule argued by another connoisseur which I will return to later.

The first literary reference to the martini that I know of is in Jack London's novel *Burning Daylight* (1910) about a man nicknamed Daylight who makes his fortune on the gold fields and goes to play the stockmarket and involve himself in other wheeling-and-dealing in Manhattan where he also learns to drink martinis.

In Manhattan, Daylight is having drinks with some of his smart new friends; it is interesting to see what they drank back in 1910. One of the men 'took mineral water served by a smoothly operating lackey . . .' while another took Scotch, while Daylight took a martini. 'Nobody seemed to notice the unusualness of a martini at midnight . . . Daylight had long learned that martinis had their strictly appointed times and places. But he liked martinis and, being a natural man, he chose deliberately to drink when and how he pleased . . .'

Even in 1910, martinis had 'their strictly appointed times and places' except, that is, for a 'natural man'.

One of my informants, Professor Hergenhan, pointed out that cocktails were drunk in Melbourne in 1870 and drew my attention to a mention in the writings of Marcus Clark to the Café de Paris in Melbourne: 'On the opposite side is the billiard room and to the right of the door leading into it a Bar where a slim, cute-looking Yankee dispenses drinks and cocktails . . .'

But we can find no reference to the martini in Marcus Clark.

The martini these days is usually drunk as an aperitif, before lunch or dinner. For a time in the US there was something called the three-martini lunch which former president Jimmy Carter condemned in 1979 as bad for the economy. He was attacking the tax-deductable, expense-account lunch; he should've outlawed it on the grounds of bad gastronomy.

When I first went to New York in 1972 some advertising people took me to a three-or-more-martini lunch at a Chinese restaurant, but apart from Voltz I know of no one who would suggest such a lunch now and would do it only to experience those days once more. It was the more creative period of American advertising but not a time of fine dining. Martinis do not go with Chinese food. The martini does not go with *any* meal. Wine goes with a meal.

That is, unless you use Nora's (Myrna Loy) approach to life in one of the *Thin Man* movies. Nora wakes up in the morning and says to Nick (William Powell), 'Pass the martinis, darling, I need breakfast.'

There are other martini-as-breakfast stories. This is how playwright Tennessee Williams' typical writing day was recorded by a companion: 'During those three days in New York with him [in 1969], living in a suite that, like all his dwellings, smelled of Listerine, I quickly became used to his routine. He arose early and made himself a martini, ordered a pot of coffee, and with a bottle of red wine in hand toddled into the living room and sat down at his portable typewriter, a battered Royal manual, and worked until noon. Then we went to lunch and later took a swim. He maintained the same schedule until he died.'

I find that drinking and writing don't mix, except for proof-reading and revising at the end of the day's work when I find it changes my focus and gives me some good results, although I always test these revisions when sober the next day.

In the first *Thin Man* film, *The Thin Man* (1934), the William Powell character believes the martini should be shaken and says that each cocktail should be shaken to a different rhythm. He says the martini should be shaken to a waltz tune.

The Manhattan cocktail, he says, is shaken to the foxtrot. The Manhattan is a relative of the martini — whisky and vermouth — and served in the same conical glass on a stem.

The Gibson is another relative of the martini — a martini served with a pickled onion instead of an olive. Gibson drinkers are a rare and strange breed. Voltz occasionally takes a Gibson. It was named after a pen-and-ink illustrator for the American magazine *Life*, Charles Dana Gibson, who died in 1940. Gibson also had a style of woman named after him, The Gibson Girl. In his drawings around the beginning of the 20th Century he was the first to depict the New Woman, on her way to early liberation – riding a bicycle, playing tennis, wearing trousers. I am impressed by a man who had both a cocktail and a style of woman named for him.

You will see that in *North by Northwest* Cary Grant is drinking a Gibson on a train (and yes, Voltz, I must admit that the glasses used in the film are quite small). In a bar a few months back I watched a girl drinking a Gibson and beside her she had a plate of pickled onions which she consumed steadily while slowly drinking her Gibson. I tried to talk with her about the Gibson but she was uninterested in the momentous tradition into which she had happily, if blindly, fallen. I left her alone. Onion after onion. She may have held martini drinkers in disdain.

When I told Voltz he became rather thoughtful and said, 'I wonder if there's anything in examining the history of pickled foods and the development of the martini. It's the only cocktail I can think of with anything pickled in it. And the Gibson.'

I said that I might look into the history of pickled foods and the cocktail.

Or I might not.

'Make a note,' he said. 'And we should know what the onions are pickled in. What in God's name is a "pickle"?'

I told him that it was either vinegar or brine, used as early preservatives, before refrigeration, as a way of keeping food from going to waste, maybe with some sweetener added.

I didn't 'make a note'.

The Gimlet – gin and fresh or bottled lime juice, served in a martini glass – could perhaps be called a distant relative, or a drink which hung out with the martini crowd. It is a drink from around the great cocktail years of the 1920s. Raymond Chandler's private eye, Philip Marlowe, drinks Gimlets.

There is the inexplicably endless argument over whether the martini is to be stirred or shaken. The phrase 'stirred not shaken' seems to be used somewhere every day by headline writers, advertising copywriters, TV and film writers, and comedians. Perhaps the people who go into these occupations have a fondness for the martini and all it stands for, or for James Bond movies which were themselves exploiting the iconic potency of the martini.

Voltz told me that he had lost a girlfriend once while at college when he asked her whether he could 'fix her a drink'. He said, 'I think it was the expression "fix a drink" which I have never used since, although it could also have been my act with the cocktail shaker – shaking it above my head. I have a theory that when men lift a cocktail shaker above their heads or when some guy at a meeting leans back with his hands behind his head, they are engaging in ape behaviour, that these postures allow the male sweat pheromones to reach the male or female in their company. A display of maleness which says "look at me, smell my power".'

It was hard to imagine a time when Voltz did not know how things were done.

'But shouldn't that work with a female? Isn't that what we are supposed to do? Aren't we supposed to give off pheromones and all that?'

I could see that Voltz did not wish to talk of the problems of men with women.

In retrospect, it explains to me why it was that Norma Crinion said to me during my martini-making lessons as a young man, when I'd put on a bartender act with the cocktail shaker over my head, 'Precious, that doesn't suit you. And anyhow the martini is stirred not shaken.'

What did she mean when she said 'it doesn't suit you'?

Some people love the sound of the ice in the shaker as part of the music of the cocktail. Norma always filled the shaker three-quarters full of ice.

Voltz had something to say about the shaking when we were in Sardi's. 'Just a few observations: Bond does indeed order his martinis "shaken, not stirred" – except in the movie *You Only Live Twice* where he conspicuously orders it the other way round. I suspect this is because the screenplay is by Roald Dahl who would know that stirring is generally the preferred technique among purists as it supposedly prevents the gin from becoming "bruised". I deviate from the purist tradition on this matter. I shake.'

I said that I had never seen the molecular evidence for this alleged bruising.

'That's your old school, Wollongong Tech – is that how you pronounce it? "Wool-on-gong?" – talking again. Let me know if you find anything under the microscope. I've always wondered if scriptwriters on the Bond films have been making subtle fun of Bond all these years by having him make the martini *the wrong way*: something a Marxist French critic would've fastened onto to deconstruct Bond's pretensions of class.'

Voltz, Master of the Ice Cube, argued that it is more effective to chill a martini down by shaking it than by stirring it.

'Take two similar glasses and put a single ice cube into the bottom of each. Now fill both with lukewarm water. Using a

34

fork, carefully move the ice cube slowly around in the glass, trying to make sure that the ice cube is able to spend some time in virtually all parts of the liquid. Have someone else put the palm of their hand over the other glass and shake it vigorously. Continue for exactly 30 seconds. Now remove the ice cubes from both glasses and stick in your finger, or better still take a thermometer reading of the water. Which is colder? The shaken glass every time.'

'Wouldn't putting the palm of a hand over the glass interfere with the result? The warmth of the palm would be conducted into the water.'

'OK, cup it with another receptacle, or a plate. Something like that.'

I then came across the famed Toronto experiment, which I duly reported to Voltz.

The Toronto Study on stirring and shaking was about its effect on the antioxidant activities of a martini. Antioxidants are thought to reduce the bad effects of ageing.

THE EXPERIMENT: Shaken, not stirred: a bioanalytical study of the antioxidant activities of martinis and hence the health value respectively of the shaken and stirred martini.

METHOD: Martinis were prepared by mixing two parts gin (6 ml) with one part vermouth (3 ml). They were either shaken vigorously (9 ml in a 100 ml medicine bottle for one minute), or stirred (9 ml in a 20 ml glass vial, using a vortex mixer).

RESULTS: Although the reason for the superior antioxidant activity of shaken martinis is not clear, is it possible that James Bond chose shaken (not stirred) martinis because of the improved antioxidant potential? This added antioxidant effect could result in a healthier beverage. The authors have not examined any antioxidant contributions from olives.

. . . the vermouth contributes more to the antioxidant properties of martinis . . . the combination of gin and vermouth is better than either gin or vermouth alone. Since much of the antioxidant activity of wine and whisky has been ascribed to the polyphenols they contain, the polyphenol content in the martinis was investigated using Folin reagent. The phenolic concentrations in the martinis . . . were in an order of magnitude lower than those in white wine or 12 year old Scotch whisky, and there was no significant difference between the phenolic contents of shaken and stirred martinis.

When I was explaining this experiment to Voltz he said that he became uneasy when I used words like 'polyphenol' and 'reagent'. 'It goes against the poetry of the drink,' he said. 'But I know it's all about your schooling in chemistry.' I'd said that at Wollongong Tech we did a lot of chemistry.

I told him that two of our Prime Ministers had been martini drinkers, that I knew of. One former Prime Minister, Malcolm Fraser, is said to take a swig of gin from the bottle, swallow it, and then pour in some vermouth to replace the gin. He shakes the bottle and then places it in the freezer for a while until cold enough to drink, then pours ready-made martinis.

'For me this crafting, while personal enough, lacks finesse, but I won't make an issue of it.' Voltz thought further, and said, 'How much exactly is in a swig?'

'An Australian swig?'

'Do you think there is a difference between an American and Australian swig?' He sounded genuinely interested.

'It wouldn't surprise me if there was.'

'You aren't being derogatory about America?'

Privately, I had thought that maybe the American swig would be larger and perhaps behind that lay a criticism of their appetites. But that would be unfair. Australians have their gluttons too.

'It would seem to me,' I said, 'that the size of the swig would have to do with the personality, but it would also have to do with the amount of vermouth you wished to introduce into the bottle.'

'I don't think it would be a cultural thing,' Voltz decided, after a moment or so. 'I agree, it is a matter of personality and vermouth judgement.'

Voltz goes further in his crafting, arguing that the vermouth and gin should each be chilled separately by shaking in ice and only then should the gin and the vermouth be combined in the glass. He refuses to give any reasoning for this.

Voltz has a friend who crafts each martini separately for each guest but he himself does not.

This brings us to the question of the lost orange bitters. Up to the 1950s orange bitters – a dash or a few drops to the glass – was sometimes added to the martini. Why this stopped is still being studied. Plays, films, books and bartenders' guides can be carbon-dated by their martini recipe. If the recipe mentions orange bitters or Angostura bitters, it comes from before 1960.

In the interests of research after finding that even the best bars no longer carry orange bitters, I went looking for it at David Jones' liquor department. While waiting to speak to the manager I overheard a conversation between him and a dapper man in his eighties.

The old man was asking about orange bitters. He wanted to buy a bottle – as I did.

I couldn't restrain myself and butted in, saying to the old man, 'Did I hear you correctly? Are you after orange bitters?'

He said that indeed he was.

'How do you use the orange bitters?' I asked the old man.

'In martinis,' he said, with a touch of impatience. 'I bought a bottle years ago, but I only use a dot or two and the bottle lasts a long time.'

I told them both I was also searching for orange bitters. The manager was astounded. 'I've never been asked for orange bitters in my twenty-five years in the liquor business. And today two people come in and ask for it at the same time!'

I looked at the older man and had an intimation of mortality. I would be him in twenty years, I would be there asking for orange bitters and behind me would be a younger man seeking the same thing.

David Jones did not stock it nor was it listed in the products offered by their suppliers. It has all but disappeared.

Bartender Leonard Opai (in Maori his name means 'all good') at the Bayswater Brasserie did find some orange bitters and we experimented with it. The orange bitters he had was a Dutch brand named Hoppe but it is a liqueur (a sweet alcoholic drink flavoured with fruits, herbs, spices, chocolate and so on) and did not work in the martini. The indefatigable Voltz tracked down the last manufacturer of orange bitters in the US, the Fee Brothers, in Rochester, New York state. Voltz said when he rang to order some orange bitters from them the woman on the other end of the telephone asked him to hold on while she 'found a pencil' to write down his order.

The Fee Brothers' orange bitters is made from water, glycerine, alcohol, and the oil of bitter oranges from the West Indies. Bitters are something of the opposite to the sweet liqueurs. The famous Angostura bitters is distilled in Trinidad, named after a town in Venezuela and allegedly uses a secret recipe of herbs and spices from 1824 when it was developed as a general purpose stomach medicine. It probably has wormwood in it.

Voltz and I tried it but decided that the last thing a martini needs is another flavour – we calculated that with vermouth and gin and the olive, not counting the wood of the toothpick or minerals in the local water, it already had more than twenty botanicals in play.

'In life that is more than enough,' Voltz said.

There is something called a Virgin martini. A woman told me that when she felt like a martini but didn't feel like drinking she'd make a shaker of ice and water with just a dash of gin, a taste of vermouth – enough to give the drink a suggestion of the martini – and add a twist. 'I drink these sometimes while reading,' she said, 'and while dreaming of a martini.'

Voltz said that you had to be open to intoxication when you drink a martini or otherwise steer well away from it. 'The martini is a pathway,' he said. 'You either take it or you don't.'

'In life, generally?'

He looked at me. 'Are you taking the piss?'

A CAPTIVATING
OBSERVATION

In my experience, the martini is the only drink that a waiter will advise you not to order because he or she does not believe that they make it properly at the bar of the restaurant in which they work.

Although, once in a Greek restaurant when Sam Dettmann and I ordered a bottle of retsina, the waiter muttered, 'Brave souls.'

THE QUESTION
OF COLDNESS

As I intimated earlier, there is even occasional dissent about the requirement of absolute coldness in a martini. One connoisseur argues that the minuscule amount of melting ice water which finds its way into the drink during the time that the gin and vermouth are together with the ice in the shaker, actually improves it. He argues that this smidgin of water is needed to give a smoothness to the ingredients and to take the 'burn' out of the alcohol.

It is true that Scotch and bourbon drinkers usually add some water, according to taste, to their drink for this reason.

I think that relieving the gin of any burn is the role of the gentler vermouth.

It is also achieved by having the martini 'on the rocks', a poetic Americanism meaning with ice. I remember that on my first trip to the US I was very resistant to American usage because I felt I would sound inauthentic if I used

Americanisms. I would not say 'on the rocks' when ordering a drink. I would say, 'With ice'. And each time the bartender would come back, 'On the rocks?' and I would be pressured into saying, 'Yes'. A martini on the rocks does mean that water increasingly joins with the drink as the ice melts. I do not find this unpleasant, although I would order a martini on the rocks only if it looked as if the drink was not going to be cold enough because of poor bar practice or when seated alfresco on a sunny day.

One problem with a martini on the rocks is that some bars will use a whisky glass to serve the martini because it needs more space for the ice. This problem is overcome by using the controversial giant martini glass.

Another connoisseur, Howard A. Rodman, is from my school of thought about coldness: 'Another crucial recommendation is that the ice be so cold and hard that it won't melt, since nothing's worse than a watery martini . . . Let me give you my personal recipe, the fruit of long experimentation and guaranteed to produce perfect results. The day before your guests arrive, put all the ingredients – glasses, gin and shaker – in the refrigerator. Use a thermometer to make sure the ice is about twenty degrees below zero (centigrade).'

He adds a refinement that I do not practice: 'Don't take anything out until your friends arrive; then pour a few drops of Noilly Prat and half a demitasse spoon of Angostura bitters over the ice in the shaker. Shake it, then pour the liquid out, leaving only the ice, which retains a faint taste of both. Then pour straight gin over the ice in the shaker, shake it again, and serve.'

When I questioned Voltz about ice and the martini when we were in Marianne's bar in New York, he was uncharacteristically embarrassed and excited. He compulsively brushed his chinos. 'I'm embarrassed to admit this, but I've discovered the way to create the perfect ice cubes for cocktails.'

Although unsettled by the demonic nature of his confession I felt I should go along with him. I asked him to describe the Voltz Ice Cube Method.

'You fill the plastic ice trays about halfway full and put them in the freezer.

'I know little about refrigeration but what I do know is that ice cubes in the tray freeze from the outside to the inside. After about an hour there's a kind of ice "shell" in the mould: ice on the outside surrounding a core of unfrozen water. You take them out at this stage.

'Then you twist the ice tray. Twisting the plastic tray seems to cause a bubble of trapped, concentrated air to float out of the water to the top of the "shell".

'I have experimented by pricking each of the semi-frozen cubes with a toothpick and then putting in more water to displace the air bubble.

'The resultant ice cubes are denser and perfect for the martini shaker or other drinks: the cubes last longer, are an interesting tone of grey, and have a heft to the tongue which is very pleasing. But I warn you, you have to work to get rid of those spider-shaped air bubbles trapped inside.'

I must have concealed my true reactions – which were to be worried about him – and instead showed interest in his ice cube method. I think I said something like, 'That's a real breakthrough, Voltz', because he looked me in the eye and put a hand on my arm. 'Thank you for being the only one of my friends to listen sensibly to my better ice-making idea. Two other friends suggested that I desperately need to get out more.'

'No,' I said, 'believe me, I understand how the idea of the perfect ice cube could capture your mind – for a time.'

Voltz says that countries can be classified by their ice. Third World ice you never touch – bad water. And there are countries without efficient refrigeration which can't get the ice hard enough.

He said that in the UK, for reasons never adequately explained, the ice is always melting and doled out by the piece, never treated with generosity or understanding.

'France doesn't understand ice – you can't buy bags of ice there.'

According to Voltz, bad ice is a very serious matter. 'When I was in St Petersburg, I was warned not to drink the water because it had a notorious bug in it. Yet I downed martinis – St Petersburg is a martini city because it is the West trapped in the East – until it occurred to me that the same dangerous water was used in making the ice cubes which had been in the shaker. So I switched to straight vodka like the rest of the locals. I think that's why Russians drink vodka straight.

'I always take warm alcoholic drinks as a sign of a not-very-advanced civilisation,' Voltz said, with intensity. 'Ice, not soap as Treitschke claimed, is the measure of civilisation. And by the way, soap can spoil a martini.'

'From bad rinsing of the glass?'

'No, on the hands. You have to be very careful not to wash your hands with strongly scented soap – in bar toilets avoid those dispensers of perfumed liquid soap; you should wash only with water, because the smell of soap on your hands will interfere with the taste of the martini. And food. You have to be careful with perfumed soap, it's a gastronomic trap.'

Going back to our discussion of ice, I told Voltz that refrigeration does not kill bacteria but it does prevent bacteria from breeding.

He said that he was glad I knew things like that. It made him feel safe in my company.

I drew his attention to the scene from the film *Basic Instinct*, in which Sharon Stone makes a drink at her beach house while detective Michael Douglas watches. She takes large chunks of ice from the fridge and violently breaks them with an ice pick (an ice pick had been used as a murder weapon in the film).

Douglas watches her forceful smashing of the ice and says, 'You got anything against ice cubes?'

Stone laughs, and says, 'I like rough edges.'

I asked Voltz where the film-makers would have found ice like that in the US. 'It's the sort of ice you get from breaking up one of those old blocks which went into ice chests.'

Apparently Voltz had given this some thought himself. 'They would have had to have it specially made by the Props Department so that she could say the line and get to use the ice pick. But I know what she means about ice. I empathise with her about that. I think that the irregular chunks of ice would expose more surface to a martini on the rocks and chill it better. I would like to see that tested. And it would give the martini an alpine look.'

I told him I had once chipped ice off a glacier in New Zealand to put in my drink. I could see by the way he looked at his college ring that he was impressed. He returned to Sharon Stone. 'Maybe we should follow that up – see where they got the ice for *Basic Instinct*?'

'I could ask my friends in the film industry. It might be worth knowing.'

I could see that we were already overloaded with investigations and that this would be low on our list.

'There is another kind of ice,' I said, 'which I would love to try in a martini. A Norwegian mariner friend who returned from the Antarctic had been scuba diving down there to make repairs to his ship. He told me that there are fine ice crystals suspended in the water. If we could devise a way of suspending the ice crystals in the martini that would be a breakthrough.'

Voltz was interested and asked questions. 'But I am loath to meddle much more with things, especially suspended things.'

'It would seem that the drink would have to be at something like minus thirty for the ice crystals to form.'

'There is a vast difference between tweaking on the way to perfection and meddling for the sake of it,' he said, closing the question for now.

I passed on Voltz's ice cube experiment by email with a martini-drinking writer friend in Paris and he replied, '. . . you and I have covered a lot of territory over the years, and visited many interesting places together and, all in all, had discussions that have ranged from the wildly amusing to the deeply depressing; we even, I recall, once went through a dumpster on a Paris street outside the old Zinc Bar then being demolished, in the deluded belief that there were precious Art Nouveau relics somehow buried inside it (why we thought this, I cannot even begin to guess, although it was after lunch).

'But nothing that we have ever discussed can compare with the valuable insights that you have provided by sending me the Voltz Ice Cube Method. Ice cube clarity; density; structure; the refracting brilliance of "treated" ice cubes compared with the cloudy patina of "free range" ice cubes. Thank you for pointing out, in such an understated and kindly manner, the risks which befall a writer after a while . . .'

I also shared it with my publisher, Jane Palfreyman, who was proposed to at the inaugural Sydney University Martini Ball and invited back the following year with her husband, David Kirk, as Mr and Mrs Martini. 'My God, where do you find these kindred souls?' she said. 'I must meet Voltz. I am ashamed to recall the countless times I have just shoved the ice tray into the freezer without a thought to the intricate aesthetic and molecular processes occurring within.'

So far the Voltz Ice Cube Method has yet to spread widely, perhaps because it requires some sense of timing and an idle life.

In New York you can buy a martini glass chiller, a balloon-shaped bowl which is designed to allow the martini glass to sit on crushed ice when it is not being drunk. Voltz is reluctant to try it, feeling that it is part of the drift towards 'gadgetry' in drinking. We agreed that such a glass holder would take away the aesthetic pleasure of the image of the martini standing on a well-polished old wooden bar.

I had the final word on coldness by suggesting to Voltz that the martini is a drink combining the paradox of both fire and ice. In the chill of the martini you find fire.

To quote the American poet, Robert Frost:

Some say the world will end in fire,
Some say in ice.
From what I've tasted of desire
I hold with those who favour fire.

My lover Paul met Robert Frost when he was at university in the US and read his work to me when we were in bed together when I was seventeen. Years later I was to read the poems of Robert Frost to my young lover while driving through Maine – the pageant of learning.

THIS THING
CALLED GIN

I first drank gin as a seventeen-year-old cadet journalist when a woman at a backyard barbecue in the western suburbs of Sydney tried to seduce me into joining the Communist Party. I was a young socialist still exploring the socialist options and had been going to Party activities including their gym class – vaulting horses and medicine balls. That was as close to being a communist as I got.

I drank too much of the gin and ended up vomiting in the garden. I never joined the Party and instead, I turned away from revolutionary socialism and the Soviet Union model and became more interested in the cooperative movement. I began describing myself as a Guild Socialist or a Cooperative Socialist, feeling that cooperative organisation should replace competitive corporations. I was then to meet up with the Sydney libertarians and non-violent anarchism which married well with my personality.

The European Union Regulation that governs spirit drinks, regulation No. 176 of 1989, defines only two legitimate gins: London gin (commonly known brands include Bombay, Tanqueray, Beefeater, Gordon's, Vickers, Gilbeys, Boodles, and, confusingly, Plymouth) and Dutch gin. Fleischmann's tried to market an American gin 'distilled from American grain' but it did not take. Other countries made gins but ultimately it is the British or Dutch gins which are drunk worldwide.

I am awaiting with interest the European Union's regulation on the exact way to make a martini. I can already see the milling crowd of expert witnesses wanting to give evidence, with many more arriving daily to appear at the hearings. I could imagine Voltz there in his long overcoat and his battered college briefcase accompanied by his lawyer.

All gins except sloe use juniper berries as a core ingredient. The juniper is a small common shrub, growing to just over a metre high, found throughout the northern hemisphere. It grows well on the slopes of the chalk downs near London, which might have given the Londoners the lead in gin-making. Juniper berries take two to three years to ripen and are then collected and laid out on shelves to dry and used for flavouring the basic alcohol.

The alcohol in gin is a white spirit made by distilling grains such as barley, corn or rye. Other flavouring ingredients, sometimes called botanicals, are then added to the grain mash during distillation. In the making of gin the juniper berries are combined with herbs and spices including coriander, angelica, orange peel, lemon peel, cardamom, cinnamon, grains of paradise (the powder of a west African spice, hot and bitter,

51

sometimes used as a drug, and sometimes chewed to warm the body), cubeb berries (an Asian shrub from the pepper family) and nutmeg.

A good gin contains six to ten botanicals mixed according to the secret recipe of each manufacturer. The gin made by Tanqueray has the odd statement on its label saying, 'made from the world's finest botanicals'.

When I pointed this out to Voltz in Campbell's bar at Grand Central Station, he thought about it in silence and then asked me if there was a hierarchy of botanicals, from poor to fine.

'I do not have a hierarchy of poor to fine in botanicals,' I said. 'We didn't have such a hierarchy at Wollongong Tech.'

'Not enough attention is given to the wording of labels. The label is a sacred document: it is the craftspeople who made the contents of the bottle talking to us, us the drinkers, us the martini drinkers. We have to be treated with respect. What we expect from a label is *straight talking*. I might write to them.'

I cannot discover where the idea that gin was a 'depressive' began. I have heard it all my life. Clinically, all alcohol is a 'depressive' in that it suppresses the responses of the nervous system but that is not what we mean conversationally by 'depressive'. We mean, a drink that makes us sad. Gin hasn't given the martini any reputation for sadness. It does not make me sad, and it doesn't take much to make me sad.

Maybe it comes from the historical association with the poor and unhappy depicted in Hogarth's drawings from the 1700s when gin was known as 'mother's ruin'. In Hogarth's Gin Alley drawings drinkers are falling over in the street, a grinning woman scratches her syphilis sores, a mother feeds gin to her baby, and in the background a person has hanged himself.

From its beginnings as a cheap drink of the poor in England, gin emerged worldwide in the 1920s as a fashionable drink along with the idea of the cocktail party.

The huge expensive yachts and privately owned small ships floating in the Mediterranean are called Gin Palaces. When Voltz stayed with me when I was living at Duke Minx's palatial house in upper Cannes, we would sit on the wide balcony with our drinks and make fun of the gin palaces. However, in some respects, we were living in a landed-mirror image of them.

In Cannes we usually drank Sidecars in homage to Scott and Zelda Fitzgerald.

Oh yes, and despite the folklore, a bottle of gin, quinine and a hot bath is not an abortifacient.

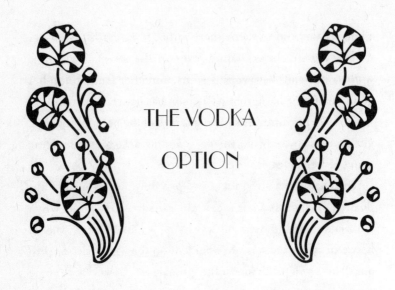

THE VODKA
OPTION

Any discussion about the martini really needs to include vodka. I realise that there are people (other than James Bond) who prefer vodka martinis.

I rush to assure you that most strict martini drinkers will allow a vodka-based martini as acceptable but I do not know when vodka martinis were first made.

Voltz, Dr Anderson and I drink vodka martinis now and then.

Vodka is a very old drink distilled from agricultural produce, traditionally from potatoes. It is considered to be odourless and colourless and is usually drunk this way, chilled in some countries but in Russia served at room temperature and straight (that is, not mixed with anything else), perhaps with a twist of lemon, and is the drink favoured by those who want not to have alcohol detected on their breath when they return to the office or to their families. Manufacturers now produce vodkas with added fruit flavours but in the basic technical sense there are no botanicals in vodka apart from the original potatoes or whatever from which it was distilled.

When I told Voltz that the writer Ian Fleming, who is generally held to be the model for Bond as well as his creator, drank martinis made from a mixture of gin and vodka he said, 'The problem with that is that it brings two strong spirits into an arm wrestle.'

'Perhaps it is a drink for those sorts of men who arm wrestle.'

'You would not, for instance, order a gin martini and then as a second, order a vodka martini.' Voltz looked at me. 'Or would you?'

'In all my life that possibility has never crossed my mind. If you had determined that your preference was for a gin martini it would be surprising if, having finished it, you decided to change path to vodka. It would have to be an exceptional circumstance.'

'Perhaps in a situation where you discovered that you had no more gin and desired a second martini.'

'But surely when you were making the first gin martini you would have determined that you did not have sufficient for the second drink?'

'You may have thought that you had a second bottle in your bar, or in the pantry, or hidden somewhere in the house.'

'It is a faint possibility. One usually knows precisely how much of what spirit is in the residence.'

'Yes, I think you are right. And anyhow the second bottle, even if found, would not be chilled. Returning to the vodka/gin martini, I guess there would be a blending occurring. Juniper marries potato. Do we know for certain if vodka is made from potatoes? What's the story on that?'

I said I would look into that. I said I had a hunch that it was no longer mass manufactured from potatoes.

He then said, 'I like the idea of it being made from potatoes. I am fond of the potato. However, the martini made from simple vodka instead of gin is a less complex martini and therefore more predictable and limited in its variations.'

I was able to tell Voltz a literary association with the combination of gin and vodka. 'The poet Robert Lowell somewhere mentions a drink he calls a Vesuvio which is gin and vodka. After the volcano. I'll get Dr Anderson to track that down.'

'It would be good to know if Lowell drank them. I thought better of him. It seems a rather coarse, drunkard's drink, which I suppose fits. Except he was a refined drunkard. Or at least that is how I wish to think of him.'

At the Bayswater Brasserie with my martini companion of many years, Dr Anderson, I raised the question of this mixture of gin and vodka and Lowell.

'I seem to remember,' he said, 'that Robert Lowell's poem "Homecoming" says something along these lines, but don't hold me to it:

At the gingerbread casino,
how innocent the nights we made it
on our *Vesuvio* martinis
with no vermouth but vodka
to sweeten the dry gin —'

We decided that Vesuvio reference was to the famous beatnik bar on the corner of Columbus Avenue and Jack Kerouac Alley in San Francisco.

Being a classicist when it comes to the martini, Dr Anderson then said to me, 'However, let's give that drink a miss.'

'I'll tell Voltz about Vesuvio and the beatnik bar, that will tickle him.'

It has, though, to be seen as a mad relative of the martini and given some degree of acceptance simply because Lowell so named it and Ian Fleming drank it.

When I conveyed this information to Voltz, he said, 'I fail to see how the vodka would "sweeten" the gin. What did the poet have in mind when he said such a thing? Is it a sweetening of the soul he talks about? I suppose even poets let their language slip now and then. Poets are supposed to try harder. I am worried about Lowell now.'

I cannot remember when I first drank vodka or who introduced me to it. When I was a cadet journalist, I remember that vodka and tonic and gin and tonic were considered as 'gay' drinks; women drank Pimms Number 1 cup – a gin liqueur and herbs, originally a 19th Century 'aid to digestion', gin and tonic, and beer shandy (beer and lemonade); beer and Scotch were seen as male drinks; and dark rum a sailors' or bushies' drink.

THE LOST
VERMOUTH

I first explored vermouth on its own – sweet and dry – with the poet Jennifer Rankin when we lived with her one-year-old boy, Thomas, in a stone hut in Bundeena surrounded by bushland on the edge of the National Park. We were both in our twenties and I was writing my second book, *The Americans, Baby*. We were interested in first getting to know vermouth as well as drinking martinis. In our financially restricted way, we were also exploring fine dining and exotic foods using my David Jones' department store credit account, a gift to me from my parents on my twenty-first birthday, on which we were living along with a small income mainly from me giving a lecture once a week at the Workers' Educational Association in the city.

We intended to pay the credit account with the advance on my book when it was finished and accepted for publication. The absence of refrigeration in the hut made our exploration of the martini and of gastronomy difficult. The hut had an old kerosene refrigerator and I worked very hard to get it back in service. Infuriatingly it froze on the first try but then died, which encouraged me to keep trying, so that just about every day I would think about the refrigerator and waste hours trying to get it going. It never froze again. Voltz often mentions this story from my earlier life and I always detect some disappointment in me for my failure to get the refrigerator going. I think he sees it as reflecting badly on Wollongong Tech for which he generally has developed a high respect.

Each week we bought a supply of food together with French wine and imported cheeses from David Jones which would be delivered to the wharf at Cronulla and then ferried across to us at Bundeena. We would lug it up the hill to our stone hut. Our introduction to game such as grouse, pheasant and so on was as imported tinned food. My friend, man of letters, and fellow martini drinker, Dr Anderson, was one of our visitors during those strange gastronomic explorations.

While living in this stone hut we had much time without company and Jenny invented and had us play out tableaus or playlets, often extending over many days, mostly with a sexual component. One she loved was Settler Family in which we would talk and act as if we were in the first Australian settlement dealing with an unknown landscape and conditions to which the bushland setting of the hut lent itself. She would like to play the convict prostitute and I had to play the role of an officer from the NSW Regiment. She also liked acting Rich Sheep Station Lady and would induce me to act as a male in pre-feminist times, which led to weird games of submission and punishment. She also developed a game called Jealous Husband where we played out being stalked and besieged by Jennifer's estranged husband. Sometimes, late at night, we would come to believe that he was out there stalking us and we would devise and rehearse escape and defence manoeuvres.

During this time Jenny and I drank martinis and played *New Yorker* Round Table at the Algonquin but without refrigeration or ice, we had to pretend that they were cold enough.

I once had a strange encounter with an earlier historical martini.

To create my character Edith Campbell Berry in my novels *Grand Days* and *Dark Palace* set in the 1920s and 1930s, I used the archives of the League of Nations in Geneva to identify some of the few women officers of her age and I then tracked their careers through the files. A young Canadian woman, Mary McGeachy, who joined the League in the late 1920s, became something of a model for Edith.

Fortunately, McGeachy was an ambitious and productive officer who made suggestions and involved herself in in-house arguments and she left lots of documents for me to trace. As I read her files, unopened for fifty or more years, her life in the secretariat began to fill my mind and to inform my book while I imaginatively created her inner life and her social life outside the office.

While I was writing and researching the book I began visiting the French town of Besançon, about two hours from Geneva, where purely by chance, I met a Canadian couple from London,

Ontario, at a dinner party at which I talked about my project and mentioned my preoccupation with this Canadian woman from the past. Almost a year after this coincidental meeting at the dinner party, a letter came from the Canadian couple saying that they had met a relative of Mary McGeachy who told them that Mary was still alive, in her nineties, and living in upstate New York.

I was confounded.

I knew that all the key players in the League of Nations had to be long dead and, because of my fictional construction and mind set, I had trouble accepting that someone from those early days of the League could still be alive. I was later to learn that Mary had put her age up to get the job with the League – as boys did to get into the army during World War I – and then put it down by seven years when she married at the age of forty.

I rang the UN Pensions department and asked them if they handled the League pension scheme and they did. I asked how many people still received a League pension. They told me only one – Mary McGeachy.

Without warning her or her family for fear of being told not to come, I flew to Keene Valley to talk with her. The family was bemused but didn't turn me away. At my first visit, Mary McGeachy was sitting in a chair in her nightdress and robe, in the living room of a timber house looking over the Adirondacks. On her lap were *Le Monde* and the *Wall Street Journal*.

I walked across the room tight with almost unbearable anticipation. I knew so much about this woman, both factually and by imaginative construction. It was hard for me to accept that she did not, in turn, know me. We shook hands, and

I dragged a chair across to be closer to her, and in my nervous-
ness dragged up the carpet with it. I must have also talked loudly
because she said, 'It's all right, my hearing is perfect.' She did,
however, apologise for her voice which was breathless and a
little roughened.

To me, Mary Craig McGeachy seemed to be an apparition.
I had studied newspaper photographs of her from the early days
and these constantly were superimposed on her face as I looked
at her then. As I began to chat with her, my mind moved in and
out of time, as, I sensed, did hers. There was an intermingling
of the real, the ghostly, and the fictional.

I felt very drawn to her and found her a becoming woman. By
touching her hand I was pulled back through the mirror of history.

Orson Welles once described this sensation to a journalist.
He reached across and took the journalist's hand. 'This hand
that touches you now, once touched the hand of Sarah
Bernhardt . . .' He went on to say that we are only about four or
five handshakes from Shakespeare.

When I shook hands with the Canadian writer Morley
Callaghan in Toronto just before he died, I thought, 'This is the
hand that knocked down Hemingway in the boxing ring in Paris
in 1929'. For a while Callaghan, Hemingway and Fitzgerald
were rated together as fine writers. Callaghan was a regular
contributor to the *New Yorker.* But then Callaghan inexplicably
fell from the pinnacle. He was so overlooked by the critics for
much of his career that Edmund Wilson thought him 'the most
unjustly neglected writer in the English language'.

One of the things I wanted to learn from Mary McGeachy was
about the social and sexual life of the young people who went to

the League. I suppose I approached it with some deference to her age. But she got my drift and said, 'Naughty girls are the best companions. I wasn't a naughty girl, I was a friend of naughty girls.' As it turned out, she was being evasive; other information I eventually came across showed that she was fairly unconventional in her love life.

Although I went to visit her to learn about those early days at the League of Nations, I found that, instead, it was I who told Mary about the life she had forgotten or couldn't recall. 'You must tell me all about myself,' she said, at one point. I also found that it became my task to tell her family about their mother's life at the League, which until then had been unknown to them.

I learned that Mary was also a life-long martini drinker but shortly after I had spent the time talking with her and returned to France, an interesting thing happened.

Her son-in-law, who both owns and runs the bar at the Keene Valley Inn, described one night, just after my visit to her, when she sent back her martini, saying it wasn't right. This surprised him because he'd been making her martinis every night for years.

He asked her what it was she wanted changed and it turned out that she wanted a martini made from dry and sweet vermouth and vodka 25:25:50. 'It was a drink I hadn't known her to have before. It seemed to have suddenly appeared out of her past.'

I had come across this drink in my research – it was a Gin Turin (albeit with vodka), a Genevan forerunner of the martini, drunk by the *bon viveurs* in the 1920s, Turin being a place where Martini & Rossi have a distillery.

When Mary asked for this drink, she was slipping back into history, through the martini glass, back into her past in the heady days of Geneva just after the War.

Perhaps by showing her documents and talking about these old days, I had returned her old life to her, and she had that night, returned there in her mind.

꙲

Some connoisseurs resist the notion that you can vary the proportions of the martini according to mood. The proportions of gin and the vermouth in the martini has provoked endless discussion.

The original mixture before the 20th Century seems to have been equal parts of gin and vermouth. Today bars serve a severely dry martini from which the vermouth is all but excluded. Most bartenders these days will swirl vermouth in the glass, then discard it, and pour chilled gin or vodka into the glass with an olive or two on a toothpick.

Some well-known martini drinkers have promoted this shift away from vermouth. Bunuel, for example, with his beam of light passing through the bottle of vermouth to strike the gin.

Hemingway mentions what he calls the Montgomery martini in his novel *Across the River and into the Trees*. A Montgomery is gin and vermouth in proportions of 15:1 — the name is a reference to the English World War II Field Marshal General Montgomery who, legend has it, would not attack without overwhelming superiority.

Some people feel that marinating the olives in vermouth is enough vermouth for the martini. I don't like this because it confuses the flavour of the olive.

My secret agenda in this book is to bring back the vermouth to the martini. It is Voltz's life's work. It is not easy.

Voltz said on the phone recently, 'Oh, and by the way, I went back to that place in Grand Central which you introduced me to, the Campbell. I ordered a martini and the bartender used a little atomiser to apply vermouth to the glass. I objected and had him make me a proper one.'

Campbell's is above Grand Central Station, the restored large private office of the early 20th Century tycoon John W. Campbell. The bar is dimly lit, with dark wooden walls and decorated with renaissance antiques, grand pianos and organs.

Voltz emailed me recently: 'There was an advertisement in the *New Yorker* this week for Grey Goose, which at last included a martini recipe that included vermouth. I believe this is a result of my letter to the company upbraiding them for not including vermouth in their Classic Martini recipe. A small triumph in the overwhelming tsunami of shit that is modern life.'

The other day I ordered a martini the way I sometimes like it: 5 parts gin to 1 part vermouth (which would be the way the *New Yorker* crowd would have drunk it in the 1930s), and the young woman bartender queried this and said, 'You want a wet martini, not a dry martini?' I hadn't heard this expression and I asked her about it. She said she'd picked it up in London. However this is a slide from the original meaning of 'dry' in the martini, which originally meant dry vermouth rather than sweet vermouth.

Again, at LA International Airport last year I tried to order a martini with the same proportions and the bartender was resistant, as if I were breaking some sacred rule. After I insisted, he accepted my order saying, 'Right. Gin, straight-up, olives and *heavy* on the vermouth.'

Connoisseur Barnaby Conrad III agrees with Voltz and I about the need for vermouth: 'The martini cocktail's clear and strong-willed simplicity is made possible by its two vigorous elements: gin for spirit and snap, vermouth for aroma and roundness.' We hold Barnaby Conrad III in high regard.

We are losing the aroma of the combination and also losing something else, the taste of wormwood, the bitter ingredient used in the preparation of vermouth. The name 'vermouth' derives from the German 'wermut' or wormwood.

Through the absence of the vermouth we have also lost the colour from the martini. In 1935, Ogden Nash, a *New Yorker* writer of light verse, who described his poetic specialisation as 'the minor idiocies of humanity' – we seem no longer to have poets who write light verse – wrote this poem about the martini:

There is something about a martini,
A tingle remarkably pleasant;
A yellow, a mellow martini,
I wish that I had one at present;

There it is, the colour of the martini in the 1930s – a yellow, a mellow martini. I sometimes like a faint yellow glint in my martini by adding more vermouth, as a sort of homage to that crowd from the 1930s. I agree, though, that there is an austere lucidity to the classic martini.

Voltz and I discovered that the yellow mellow martini is reached by adding .12 vermouth to every one part of gin. We are both more inclined to the lustre of .2 vermouth.

Dry vermouth is created by infusing wine (French vermouth is made from white wine grapes) with herbs, spices, barks and peels, then allowing it to mature. Vermouth is first recorded in the 1700s and became internationally known through the Italian company, established by Sig. Martini and Sig. Rossi, and the French company Noilly Prat, established by M. Noilly and M. Prat, which was the vermouth preferred by Ernest Hemingway.

The name of the cocktail almost certainly comes from the name of the Italian vermouth makers Martini & Rossi. We may as well deal with the origin of the drink now. The gin comes from London, the vermouth from Italy or France, the olive from the Middle East. No one is sure where the design of the glass came from. The combining of these ingredients almost certainly went on in any place where London gin and Italian or French vermouth were available and where the drinkers were playful. The cocktail hour came from the idea of the European aperitif. The glamour came from the Americans.

Sadly, these days in Europe, outside the finer bars, when you order a martini you are often served simply a glass of chilled Martini & Rossi vermouth.

Why wasn't it called a Rossi? Rossi probably asked himself that question until he died.

I came across one of the best descriptions of the place of vermouth in a martini in the crime novel *B for Burglar* by Sue Grafton. '[My martini] was silky and cold with that whisper of vermouth that makes me shudder. I always eat the olive early because it blends so nicely with the taste of gin. He caught sight of my shiver. "I can leave the room if you want to be alone with that."'

The presence of wormwood in vermouth excites the romantics because it links the martini with the legendary drink absinthe, made famous by writers and painters who mythologised the drink: Manet, *The Absinthe Drinker* (1859), Degas, *L'absinthe* (1876), Jean-François Raffaëlli, *The Absinthe Drinkers* (1881), Vincent van Gogh, *Still Life with Absinthe* (1887) and Picasso's *Buveur de l'absinthe* (1901).

In 19th Century Europe, absinthe had a reputation for causing hallucinations and dangerous behaviour. The early impurity of some of the absinthe made then led to bad side-effects and it was banned in France in 1915. In recent years, the drink has been cleaned up and has made a comeback among romantics. The alcohol content of the original absinthe was very high.

Because of the wormwood, absinthe was a very bitter drink and had to be sweetened with sugar. As you might expect, Voltz is an absinthe romantic and he told me in Cannes: '... evidently there are quite a few absinthe spoons. Mine looks like a little garden shovel or the sort of thing with which you pick up pieces of cake – except it has holes in the shape of stars to permit the absinthe to flow through the sugar cube. There is also a type which looks like a very long spoon. There are also, from what I can tell, about a half dozen types of absinthe glasses . . . By the way I had luncheon on Saturday with Reinaldo Herrara, famous Venezulean socialite. He brought his strapping young trainer along, although for what reason I couldn't begin to tell you. Perhaps when you reach a certain age and sophistication you like to be accompanied by someone, no matter who, when you go to town. We ate at Lupa's, an excellent new Italian restaurant. I haven't tried the absinthe martini, but I'm growing more interested . . .'

Wormwood is a shrub found in Europe and North America. It gives the bitter taste to the aniseed drinks made from dill or anis, such as Pernod, which was invented in 1797 by M. Henri-Louis Pernod, and pastis and ouzo, and was also used traditionally as a medicine before becoming a social drink.

Professor Brian Kiernan – himself not a martini drinker – first brought my attention to the startling fact that people in the 1950s would add a dash of the insecticide DDT to their cocktails. I found it hard to believe, even if there have been times in my life when I was willing to swallow just about anything if it promised a good time.

However, when I came to look at the molecular structure of DDT and wormwood, I found, strangely, that they are very close indeed and that historically wormwood was used as an insect repellent.

Voltz was unsettled by this historical fact and, I suspect, dismissed it as what he sometimes refers to as 'Wollongong chemistry'.

It was also Professor Kiernan who sent me the 1920s quotation from Somerset Maugham about the absinthe martini:

'. . . the manservant brought in a tray with an array of bottles and Isabel, always tactful, knowing that nine men out of ten are convinced they can mix a better cocktail than any woman, asked me to shake a couple. I poured out the gin and the Noilly Prat and added the dash of absinthe that transforms a dry Martini from a nondescript drink to one for the gods of Olympus . . .'

Professor Kiernan is best known among drinkers for the Kiernan Fallacy — that at a restaurant dinner expensive high-quality wines are cheaper because they are drunk slowly.

A DISTURBING OBSERVATION

To: Voltz@aol.com
Subject: a disturbing observation

Voltz, I have discovered a dry-cleaning company that uses the business name 'Dry Martini' together with the classical martini glass signage as its logo. I could take this to the Business Names Commission or I could put a brick through the window. Obviously, it is disturbing. Weeks afterwards, at the cocktail hour, I still find myself thinking of dry-cleaning fluid in a martini glass. Not a palatable image.

From: Voltz@aol.com
Subject: a disturbing observation

In America, there's a dry-cleaning process called 'Martinizing'. I wonder if your dry-cleaner is playing off of that or has just misunderstood it? This process is named after its inventor, a Mr Martin.

Could it be the company you refer to is using gin and vermouth as a cleaning fluid?

THE BREAST: THE
BRA: THE GLASS

As we know – in the sense that we know rain beating on a tin roof – Voltz believes that the martini is at present served in glasses that are too large. He dismissively describes them as 'buckets'.

Once in the bar of the Ritz in London, he said to me, 'I was watching an old Humphrey Bogart movie from 1942, *All Through the Night*, and at one point Bogart is at a nightclub and orders a sherry for his girlfriend and a "double martini" for himself. The drinks are delivered in nearly identical-sized glasses: this tells me that a "double martini" in the 1940s meant a drink only as large as a stemmed sherry glass. Most of the drink was actually taken up by the olive. I am continuing my campaign to return to smaller martinis . . .'

I agreed that the smaller glass does not have time to warm in the hand.

Through the intricacies which go to form taste and preference in design, the martini evolved its own glass: a clear, conical vessel (leaving aside the question of size for now) on a stem which keeps the warm hand away from the drink. Glass manufacturers' catalogues from the 19th Century show glasses approximating the martini glass but Voltz and I cannot track down the name of the designer.

The martini glass is celebrated in cocktail lounge signage throughout the world; that beckoning sign of the neon-lit martini glass often with a neon olive in it, sometimes flashing on and off outside a cocktail lounge or at an airport bar. I have found that after driving all day in the US and arriving in a strange city, this flashing neon martini makes me want to stop and go into the bar, especially those windowless American bars sometimes found on the highway strip on the way into the central business district of a city.

The neon martini glass always promises relief from the discomfort of being alive. And often gives it. I share the philosophy of Blanche in Tennessee William's play *A Streetcar Named Desire*: 'I have always relied on the kindness of strangers' – and in my case, the tranquillity of the martini. At least, that is, I shared Blanche's philosophy until I saw *Angels in America* and heard Jeffrey Wright (Belize) say, 'Well, that would be a foolish thing to do.'

So ubiquitous is the martini glass that the New South Wales State Railways have as their 'No Drinking on Trains' sign a martini glass with a bar across it. I have never seen a martini drunk on a New South Wales train nor have I seen a bar car. I dream of the day when the martini glass symbol is there with a tick beside it and an arrow pointing to the bar car.

When I mentioned this to Voltz last year he took me to a park on 6th Avenue in New York City where the martini glass with a bar across it is used as a sign forbidding alcohol. Voltz said, 'It is as if the park authorities fear that Nick and Nora and their friends will invade this park for a cocktail party. Or that the old Algonquin crowd will stroll down and take over.'

Once when I was living out of New York City in Westchester, I would sometimes take the commuter train from Grand Central Station; on the platform near the doors to the train would be a man seated at a table with ice and premixed martinis and a stack of large paper cups. The commuters would buy their double or triple martinis from the man in paper cups filled with ice and take them onto the train to sip on the journey home. I suppose many would also be greeted by a freshly made-up wife with another martini already made for them and she would play the piano while they talked about their day (at least, that was how I imagined married life then). Stylistically, the paper cups disappointed me and I considered the whole practice a grave offence against the dignity of the martini, but it sure as hell affirmed the centrality of the martini in that commuter culture described so well by John Cheever.

Any drinking vessel is a technological artefact which evolved from the cupped hands, from the time our forebears squatted at a stream to scoop up water to drink with their hands. I guess one day some smart forebear started using a pod or a nut or shell or an animal horn and then began to carve and fashion a cup, which quickly led them back to the shape of the female breast which, for most of us, was our first drinking vessel. Those needing mysticism were also quick to use the cup, renamed a 'chalice' as a central spiritual symbol. There is something called a double-cup which has been used in some ceremonials over the centuries. The two parts of the cups fit together and can be broken apart. Each person drinks from a section of the double-cup in a celebration of their bonding. In some ceremonies it was thought special toasts from these cups would make women fertile and men virile. I suppose in some more secular bondings the women silently toast in the hope that the men will, at least on that night, remain virile but that they will be, for that night, infertile.

There are many bar legends about the shape of glasses and the shape of breasts.

Two of the most common are that Madame de Pompadour, mistress of France's Louis XV, had glasses crafted in the shape of her breasts as a gift for Louis because he admired her breasts and he wanted to be able to drink champagne from them. There is another legend that the dish-shaped champagne glass was designed for Louis XVI and was shaped from Marie Antoinette's breast.

It seems to me that the martini glass derives from the breast-shaped tradition of glass design, perhaps by way of the cone-shaped bra found in early Eygptian paintings. Some depictions of Cleopatra show her in such a bra. The conical bra was fashionable for a time in the 1920s and then again in the 1950s, when it was marketed as a whirlpool bra and can still be bought and which is something of a festish object. Jean-Paul Gaultier designed what he called a 'cone bra' for Madonna as part of a corset called the *classique* for her Blonde Ambition tour in 1990.

If you would like to make one of these corsets for yourself, the middle panel on the costume is actually made from ribbons that are woven together to make a diamond pattern effect. If you have the patience, certainly try doing this as I did on my first Blondie costume. But if you want to get the costume finished faster then take the quilting route which is more efficient and produces the same effect. Fuseable batting and a ruler to draw the lines for the stitch work are some of the tools you'll need.

Just kidding.

Gaultier markets an eau de toilette in a bottle shaped as the figure of a woman wearing the *corset classique.*

I have never said this to Voltz, but I have a feeling that his desire to return to some vaguely visualised, ideal smaller glass from times past may be a hankering after the primal nipple. Maybe it's time I did. The glass he dreamily describes to me seems to shrink from the breast-size ever closer to the nipple-size. He once said to me in the bar of the '21' Club that he sometimes hankers after the almost thimble-size glasses of the 1920s. I let it pass.

Instead, I have repeatedly told him that the Greeks preferred wide goblets or bowls because they claimed that the more of the mouth that is exposed to the liquid, the fuller the sensation. They were right, because the wide rim not only exposes the lips to the liquid but also the nose, which is intrinsic to taste. The martini glass is perfectly designed to maximise the sensation to the lips and to the nose.

The adjectives modernist and moderne (from the Latin word *modo* meaning 'just now') are applied to the martini and its glass by Max Rudin in an essay 'There Is Something About a

Martini', in an issue of *American Heritage* magazine. By these words I understand him to mean the geometric Art Deco period, which he sees as coming to an end with World War II and from which the conical or triangular cup of the martini glass with its straight line stem and disc base is an example. Perversely, my favourite martini glass, purchased in a second-hand shop in Cannes, has an Art Nouveau, more organic stem that resembles tangled flower stalks.

A young woman at my lecture on the martini in Shanghai last year suggested that the strange drinks that are emerging and claiming to be variations on, or parodic departures from, the classic martini and that are served in martini glasses are post-modern, which embraces everything from the past and playfully mucks around with it. What Voltz calls The Crazy Drinks, in fact, poke fun at the staidness of the classic martini as a representative symbol of a fading modernism.

I would argue that The Crazy Drinks also inescapably pay homage to the martini, especially when they steal its glass.

Be that as it may.

Actually, unlike Voltz, I do not deride The Crazy Drinks, the post-modern drinks, and I am curious enough about them to taste them when a companion orders one. The thing of it is this: *I just haven't time enough to include them in my life.* Inclusion at best is an act of appreciation, and appreciation has its sometimes tiring demands. To be honest, I have enough trouble coming to terms with all the potential in the martini and its close relatives without straying away from it to other drinks.

Let's get one thing straight: the martini glass can vary slightly but should not stray too far from its traditional shape. The drinker of classic martinis does not, for example, admit the zig-zag stem which is the signature glass of a cocktail lounge called Twist at the Ameritania Hotel in Manhattan, which serves drinks in large cone-shaped glasses with 'Z' shaped stems. Voltz and I have banned this bar.

This is sometimes known as the Shazam Stem, which is taken from the signature lightning bolt of the comic strip character Captain Marvel, published between 1939 and 1953. In his everyday life, Captain Marvel was Billy Batson, child reporter for Whiz radio, who became a superman-style hero when he said the word 'shazam'.

Twist specialises in The Crazy Drinks such as the Espresso Chocolate Martini or the Times Square Tootsie.

Which reminds me that at the premiere party of the now-concluded TV series 'Sex and the City' in 2000, one of the stars of the show, Sarah Jessica Parker, requested 'a fun, pink drink' from the bartender. According to *Men's Journal*, the drink that was served to her could be described as a feminist manifesto (but did not explain why): it was raspberry syrup, 'Razberi' Stolichnaya vodka, Cointreau, lime, pineapple and cranberry juices, with a splash of champagne and served in a large martini glass. Parker named it the Flirtini. The magazine said it was a 'chick drink' because of its colour, fruitiness and sweetness – 'as pretty to look at as it is easy to drink – with the alcohol well disguised'.

Whatever this Flirtini was, despite the homage of its name, it is nowhere near, or even related to the martini. Nor was the favourite drink of the women in the TV series, The Cosmopolitan – vodka, Cointreau, lime and cranberry juice –

which is perhaps a good drink in itself but not a relative of the martini. Why doesn't this Sarah Jessica Parker and her friends who like these drinks find their own glass and leave the martini glass alone?

Voltz told me that in New York City there is on sale a stemless martini glass: the conical portion is kept upright when not in use by setting it in a special globe packed with crushed ice. I said to him that the International Martini Glass Design Competition to which I was invited (I voted for no change in the shape of the glass), had as one of its finalists an oystershell-shaped glass which worked the same way – it rested on a bed of ice.

I became excited because these stemless, footless glasses resemble the original 'tumbler', the word we sometimes use for a basic drinking glass.

At Delmonico's (a place he detests but which has history), I was able to tell Voltz that drinking glasses were once made with a rounded bottom but with no handle or foot and so that they would not stand upright – they would tumble.

'Why were they made like that?'

I said that it had to do with the limitations of rudimentary glass blowing, but I really didn't know. 'It had to be drunk before it could be put back down on the table. It was a ceremonial thing.'

'I suppose you did a lot of glass blowing at Wool-loo-mo-gong Tech.'

'Wollongong. The tumbler is a Wollongong ceremonial drinking glass.'

I told Voltz that Pepys had two tumblers made from silver.

Eventually a tumbler holder was invented just like the martini chillers we had been describing.

'Where's the glass-blowing in these silver tumblers of Pepys? I suspect the name comes from the tumbles of the drinker, and sometimes I believe that you story-tell some of this stuff. I doubt the glass-blowing story.'

He was right. I have no idea why tumblers were first made in that shape.

Voltz brightened up and said, 'I seem to remember that Pepys liked the word "tumble" to describe sexual pleasure. If my memory serves me well, he and a girl went to "a stable by the Dog tavern, and there did he tumble her and toss her".'

'Yes,' I said, 'it's my recollection that "tumble" was one of Pepys' favourite words for sexual pleasure.'

'We'll always use the word "tumbler" now,' Voltz declared. 'In honour of Pepys and in honour of sexual pleasure.'

'Yes. We won't say glasses or beakers.'

'No. Just "tumblers" from now on.'

Martini traditionalists do not admit a glass flecked with colour, and, as Voltz incessantly points out, nor do we approve of the fashion for the giant glass.

Though I have come across a martini glass with a gold rim and I am of two minds about this and can imagine an argument for it. The use of gold in design is always suspect because of its connection with wealth, ostentation, money-sickness, gold bath taps and gold toilet seats. However, the gold-rimmed glass could be seen as a design echo of the 'yellow mellow martini' and as a tilt towards a respectable and sound sense of splendour.

There is the legendary Algonquin cobalt-blue martini glass, not used in my time at the Algonquin and which I have never seen, which I guess we have to accept out of literary respect for the Round Table crowd who drank from these glasses. The problem is that it deprives the martini of its cold, transparent lucidity.

The diligent Voltz continues with his search for the 'right-sized martini glass'. He once wrote: '. . . I'm just back from London. I stayed at the Savoy, which as you know has a good "American Bar" renowned for its martinis – this time I noticed that they now serve them in little, tulip-shaped glasses, which feel like something they found in the attic in the 1920s and seem to me to be just right. To change the subject, I went to Tiffany's last week to buy a friend a wedding present, and was distinctly disappointed with the quality of their cocktail glassware. Expensive stuff, yet lacking in the kind of under-stated shape and cut you want from a good highball or whiskey glass. I've had much better luck at a place called Fish's Eddy, which sells seconds and discontinued glasses from old restaurants and hotels.'

I was interested in Voltz's mention of the American Bar at the Savoy where I often drink with my agent Derek Johns. American bars in Europe once imitated those American bars from the old movies but are now generally odd places where the women in the bar are paid to use their sexuality to encourage men to buy expensive drinks. They border on prostitution but, in my experience, the sex on the premises is restricted to touching and limited cuddling. No lap dancing though.

Another challenge to the classic martini glass is the Hongell glass made familiar by Hitchcock's film *The Birds* (1963). The martinis are served in a glass that is wide at the rim and then narrows down slightly to a heavy heel or base – no stem. Voltz will not discuss it.

Camille Paglia, one of my favourite social theorists, disappointed me when she said of the film, 'Hitchcock sculpts the human body in space . . . I love the way Tippi [Hedren] handles cigarettes and a martini glass with such remarkable sophistication. It is gesturalism raised to the level of choreography.'

My disappointment is that Paglia should've unthinkingly accepted the glass used in the film as a 'martini glass'. It is not a martini glass. True, they say that they are drinking martinis but the glass is aberrant.

Hitchcock not only discovered Tippi Hedren but also put this aberrant martini glass into Tippi's hand. Because of the popularity of the film it is now known as the Tippi glass and sold as such.

Glass designer Goran Hongell, one of the pioneers of the Finnish glass tradition in the 1950s, designed the glass. Hitchcock discovered Hongell's martini glass at the Ritz Bar in London and bought some to take back to his home in the US, but also decided to use two of these glasses in *The Birds*. As it is, the Hongell glass is my preferred picnic glass because it can be used outdoors for a diversity of drinks including wine but never for martinis. Its heavy base is ideal for resting on the ground or on grass and it keeps it from tumbling.

Perhaps the holding of a martini glass is part of our own 'gesturalism', and becomes part of our own image when we are seated in a bar holding a martini – what I call the *affiliation awareness* in the drinking of the martini. Perhaps, when holding a martini, we are fleetingly relocated into a scene composed of all the films, cartoons and books from which we have learned of the martini – perhaps we become part of a psychological image not of our own making, but one we've earned the right to inhabit if our attitude to life and to the martini are right. We become momentarily conscious of our part in a historical continuity; we are for a second or two partly embedded in its imagery. This in turn releases us a little from the reality of our own personality, glamorises us a little. As we hold the martini we join a great and wonderful crowd from the past.

By the way, the Austrian glass company Riedel has seventy styles of drinking glass, including a 5oz martini glass (less than half the size of a Twist martini glass but not small enough to make Voltz happy) and glasses for grappa and for water. Voltz says that the gauge of a sophisticated household is the number of glasses it possesses which are appropriate to the beverage. I agree.

THE OLIVE AND
THE LEMON TREE

In my 'Martini' story, the eighteen-year-old girl, drinking her first martini which the older man had just mixed, pauses to admire the beauty of the drink, and observes that the olive on the toothpick gives the drink an axis.

He had never before observed this. She has taught him something in return.

She also asks what she should do with the olive: 'Do you eat it at the beginning or the end of the drink or is it just a . . . garnish?'

I now remember a note from a sassy, martini-drinking woman friend which read, '. . . it's a long slow day after an evening of (gin) martinis. I felt it important to practise the art of cocking the tail to ensure that I would remember how to drink elegantly and appropriately for when we catch up. But I was in trouble from my companion for eating all the olives and not leaving one in my glass until the drink was drunk. I am clearly out of practice as well as out of sorts.'

Without consulting Voltz, I rang her back immediately to tell her that the leaving of one olive in the martini was a purist position – some argue that the olive should not be eaten, that it is purely a visual pleasure. I told her that this line is pushed by the American Standard Dry Martini Club; also *Tin House* magazine in NYC argues that one olive should be left until the end in their own specially designed martini. I said I knew of no such universal rules concerning the olive. It is only in recent years that bartenders have put more than one olive in a martini – I have seen up to five, but this then requires a larger glass and pushes the martini towards being a snack. The Bloody Mary also went through a phase of being loaded up with vegetables, celery and so on.

It seems to me that you may eat up the olives any old way: meditatively, impulsively, unthinkingly – although, oddly, this goes against the central tradition of the martini, that it is a drink about which nothing relating to it is done unthinkingly.

The other quandry of having more than one olive is that if it is unpitted, the toothpick has to be pushed through the olive to avoid the pit. This is fine with one olive and keeps the aesthetic of the martini. More than one and you end up with a toothpick and a lopsided string of olives. Of course with stuffed olives, the toothpick can be centred and the resulting formation of olives looks correct.

As the man explains in the story, some people like to prick the olive with the toothpick and watch the oil seep out into the drink. But you should not sit at the bar spending too much time pricking the olives in a martini and watching the oil seep out. You will attract worried attention.

When I was living with Sarah Ducker and her son Harry, who was about six, he would enjoy mixing the martinis at the cocktail hour. He would have a juice and I would have a martini while we watched the television news. During one mixing he misremembered my instructions and put the olives in the martini shaker rather than the glass. After he had finished his mixing, we fished them out of the cocktail shaker and put them in the martini glass. It was, accidentally, an acceptable innovation to the martini. From then on we called this martini a 'Harry Catterns' and now years later I sometimes make my martini this way in memory of the good times we had together. If he can still remember how to make a martini, that is a fine continuation of the pageant of learning, from Norma through me to Harry – a stretch of more than fifty years.

Hundreds of cartoons have appeared about the martini – especially in the *New Yorker* magazine which began in 1926 when the martini began to assert itself as the cocktail of taste and discernment. It was best known as the drink of the Algonquin Hotel Round Table lunching club, established in the 1920s, made up of writers from the *New Yorker* and other literati, although the Round Table predates the *New Yorker*. Dorothy Parker was one of its better known members. The Round Table is recreated in the film *Mrs Parker*, where Dorothy is played by Jennifer Jason Leigh.

My proudest moment in martini drinking was when I returned to the old Blue Bar at the Algonquin after two years' absence. The only person in the bar, I seated myself on a stool, having just arrived from a twenty-five-hour flight from Australia. Without looking around, Dave Gresham, the bartender, Vietnam vet, a fan of my books, who was polishing glasses (as an idle bartender should — according to Dave to remove any detergent residue) said, 'Bombay gin, Noilly Prat the old way, straight-up, two stuffed olives — right, Moorhouse?' He had seen me in the mirror.

It was a Sunday evening and pouring with rain and after an hour no one else had come into the bar. Dave went to the door and put up the closed sign and we settled in for a night of drinking. There in the old Blue Bar of the Algonquin, we were visited by some great ghosts including, of course, Dorothy Parker, John Cheever, Harold Ross and others. I think the bar had originally been located in another part of the lobby area but the ghosts found us all right.

Many things about the martini garnish are argued in pursuit of perfection — olive pitted or unpitted, stuffed or unstuffed, olive or a twist of lemon peel, or whether a drop of brine from the olive jar improves the martini or whether it makes something else called, positively, a 'dirty martini'.

In the bar of the White Horse (where Dylan Thomas died), I once asked Voltz about the dirty martini.

'I am sure that the dirty martini seems to be a name given to something that came about by accident,' he said. 'Often when olives are added to martinis, a little brine from the olive jar gets into the drink from the olives, sometimes more than at other times. Someone, somewhere decided to call it a dirty martini and to intentionally put in a little more brine than would normally come off the olives. Hardly a rage here in New York where The Crazy Drinks are in fashion, although I want to believe they're dying out.'

We discussed whether in the mixing of a dirty martini, the brine should go into the shaker rather than the glass.

Voltz replied quite sensibly that there would always be some brine in any martini from the olives and to add more brine into the shaker at the mixing was a tricky business. 'It requires a developed sense of judgement. And some dexterity. You have to be aware of how much has gone into the shaker and then pre-calculate how much might get into the drink when the olives go into the glass, which in turn depends on who is handling the olives, whether they are a sloppy sort of person or not. There is a certain sloppy style which I don't mind as long as it flows from a generous personality and not from carelessness.'

Voltz said that he did not believe in using the product now marketed as 'olive juice'. There is an olive juice made from the crushed leaves of the olive tree but this is not what we are talking about. And do not add pure olive oil to a martini.

'When Roosevelt met with Winston Churchill and Joseph Stalin in Tehran in 1943 . . .' I offered.

'Ah,' he said. 'Tehran.' Voltz shook his head at my having teasingly and slyly held back the evidence for my nomination of Tehran as a martini city.

'. . . Roosevelt, Churchill, and Stalin were in Tehran discussing the end of the war. It was there that they agreed to create an international organisation to maintain the peace – the UN.'

'Come on – out with your arcane knowledge.'

'Patience. Roosevelt served each of them his favourite dirty martini, which was two parts gin, one part vermouth, and a splash of olive brine.'

'Very good.' He made a noise resembling a chuckle, for he rarely chuckles. 'Tehran is in.'

'Yes. Tehran is, I think, possibly a martini city for this reason alone.'

'But,' he said, 'not having been to Tehran I would suspect that one would have to bring one's own ingredients and make the drink oneself. However, I agree that it would be historically obtuse to visit Tehran and *not* drink a dirty martini.'

I pointed out that Roosevelt's proportions of vermouth and gin were those of the 1930s and 1940s, although I would have expected his martini to contain a drop or two of orange bitters which was part of the martini back then. But Roosevelt had gone to the trouble to take his martini makings with him to Tehran and it is unlikely that he would have forgotten the orange bitters, so he must have abandoned it by then.

'I am unsure about the "splash" of brine,' Voltz said. 'That seems to me to be too much. A half-splash would also seem a lot. Maybe a flick or two of brine per glass would be right, though flicking is always a ticklish business.'

'I have known people to use an ounce of brine for two martinis.'

'That is wrong. That would topple the martini over into something else.'

'Is there a difference between a splash and a dash?'

'From what I remember from my mother's *Country Women's Association of NSW Cookbook* a dash is a sixth of a teaspoon.'

'Are all teaspoons the same size then? In Wollongong?'

'Yes. And I think that the word splash is longer than the word dash, which suggests that a splash is larger than a dash.

Not much larger. That's what's known as the Lexicographer's Measure.'

'It seems to me that the dash has more force to it, less control; you are likely to get more from a dash than from a splash.'

'No, you're wrong about that. Splash is bigger. But I do know that both are less than an ounce.'

'I think that in future it's wise to always ask a bartender if he's using a dash or a splash and what his measure is.'

'Yes.'

'And a flick. A flick is less than a dash.'

'Yes.'

'But it has more letters in it than dash – what about the so-called Lexicographer's Measure?'

'Flick is a *thin* word. Dash is a fat word. It goes flick, dash, splash.'

'It's a tricky business.'

I was also able to tell Voltz that after signing the act repealing Prohibition in 1933, Franklin Roosevelt celebrated by mixing the first legal martini in the White House.

'And I have another Roosevelt martini-diplomacy story.'

'Yes?'

'Legend has it that when they met again in Yalta in 1945, Roosevelt again made a martini for Stalin. He'd wanted to serve it with a twist but had forgotten the lemons. He apologised to Stalin. Next morning Roosevelt woke up to find a lemon tree with two hundred lemons on it outside his residence there in Yalta. Stalin had had a lemon tree up-rooted from his native Georgia and flown in overnight and replanted.'

Voltz looked startled. 'You mean that Roosevelt made a dirty martini with olive brine and then put in a *twist*?'

I hadn't thought about that. 'Well, I guess, yes.'

Voltz was doubtful. 'I don't know about mixing olive brine with a lemon twist.'

'I'm not absolutely sure that Roosevelt was still making dirty martinis in 1945. Maybe he'd changed his mix.'

'You aren't suggesting that Yalta is a martini city nominee?'

'I am not familiar with Yalta. As a city, that is. It is really just a martini anecdote. I am not pushing Yalta.'

'Good. I wouldn't think of Yalta as a martini city. Tehran is in – just – because it is the *first* example of martini diplomacy.' Voltz then frowned. 'Do you know what worries me about the Yalta Lemon Tree story?'

I ran through it in my head. 'Yes, I do. It's the two hundred lemons. The precision of the count. Right?'

'Right. Legendary stories often include those sorts of precise details. As authentication. Who counted them? Roosevelt? Did he stand there in the snow and go "one-two-three-four" up to two hundred?'

'It was December. The ground would've been frozen like rock. There is no way they could've even planted that tree.'

'They could've blown a hole in the ground – yeah.'

'And even so, was Roosevelt going to stand there counting them? Or did some aide count them? If so, why?'

'Discount that story. And another thing – I seriously doubt you can fit two hundred lemons on a tree. But you could check that.'

'Why me?'

'You're the one who does the checking.'

'Not this time. You know that with a dirty martini it is not only brine that you get in your martini,' I continued. 'In the liquid you get water, salt and some lactic acid which is commonly used in foods, sometimes as a flavouring, but it also reduces the risk of salmonella. Lactic acid comes from lactose, the sugar in milk, and is found in sour milk — remember that sour-sweet taste when you discover that the milk has turned? It is used to make yogurt and cottage cheese. When we exert ourselves physically we make lactic acid. You can taste it in the mouth after a run.'

'*You* might.' He pondered. 'I've never tasted this lactic acid of which you speak, in a martini.'

'I am not saying that it would be tasted. It would blend.'

'The presence of that lactic acid does not meet with my full approval but I suppose it is unavoidable. At least in the way you describe it. And I suppose it has always been there. Undetectably. Is it *there* if it's undetectable?'

'Chemically there but not *consciously* there.'

Voltz thought about this. 'I suppose that can be said about other ingredients that become blended.'

'I suppose it is the distinction between a compound and mixture.'

'Wollongong Alchemy. Again.'

'A mixture has ingredients that do not change when they are mixed, say oil and water. In a compound, however, when they interact with each other, they change to form a new thing.'

'Is the martini, then, a mixture or a compound?'

'A mixture of mixtures and compounds. Alcohol is a compound.'

'We should look into that. Should follow that up further. At some point. Just so that we are clear about it. I want to be absolutely clear about it.'

'If I have an objection to the dirty martini, it would be that the drink loses lucidity. It becomes slightly clouded. And, of course, its salinity rises.'

Voltz frowned. 'I wonder if the salt in the brine is rock salt from salt mines, pond salt, or sea salt?'

'I suppose it depends on which town in which country the salting of the olives takes place.'

'It might be worth looking into that at sometime.'

'Yes. Maybe.'

Voltz then became worried. 'Damn it, now we have iodised salt, so the brine will have iodine in it. I wonder if that changes the martini. It must make it taste different from the martinis they drank before salt was iodised.'

'I'm sure it does. Actually it's potassium iodide.'

'It's good to know things like that. I suppose it's possible to find non-iodised salt.'

'It's worth looking into. The French also put fluoride into their salt.'

'Damn. We have to find our way back to pure salt.'

'And get thyroid problems from lack of iodine?'

'There must be other ways of avoiding thyroid problems and bad teeth, other than screwing around with the salt?'

'I hear that they've found salt on Mars.'

'That might be very good salt. There's a business opportunity in that. We should try to get hold of some of that Mars salt.'

'What are our chances, do you think?'

'I have friends in NASA. I could give it a try.'

'What if it turned out to be Mars-salt-plus X?'

'And we grew tails?'

'Something like that. You can try it first.'

The twist of lemon in a martini is accepted as an alternative to the olive. The lemon rind is twisted to cause the lemon oil to spray onto the drink – the zest of the lemon, *un zeste de provocation* – but usually it is a piece of lemon rind dropped into the drink. At Sardi's bar in New York, the old barman squeeze-sprayed the lemon oil so well you could see it on the surface of the drink – what Kurt Vonnegut Jnr calls the 'dancing myriads of winking eyes'.

At the Water's Edge in Canberra, the martini-maker rubs the lemon peel around the rim of the glass which strengthens the presence of the lemon.

Some bartenders make a snake out of the rind, some tie it in a bow, although some drinkers feel this is getting too close to the problem of overtouching of food. Voltz and I praise the crafting of the lemon twist as evidence of *deliberation*.

There was a lemon tree in our garden when I was a child. Many Australians grew up with a lemon tree in the backyard, often the only fruit tree in the garden. The lemons from our tree had a lumpy skin and thick white rind and were known as Rough Skins. As a child I tried many times to make lemonade from these lemons using the *Country Women's Association of NSW Cookbook* but it was never 'right' because it was not carbonated.

By then my ideal lemonade was the commercial soft drink. I never sold it from a jug on a table at the front of the house for 1 cent a glass, as I had seen it done in comics and films, but it did cross my mind.

At around the age of eight or nine, I moved out of my family home and set up house in a huge box under the lemon tree. I took my books and some toys and possessions into my new home. My first and only real home. I think my family was glad to see me go. My memory is that I stayed there at least two nights and that eventually rain forced me to take everything back into the house despite the metallic foil lining of the box which I had thought would waterproof it.

I ran away from home a couple of other times before I ran away to the city for good at sixteen years and ten months to become a copyboy on a newspaper.

From martini drinkers in bars around the world I have learned that lemons were originally found in China and Northern India and then spread to nearly every country of the world. The Lisbon and Eureka are the most common commercial lemon, very regular in shape, with a bright yellow smooth skin and a tangy taste and a pointed nipple-like end.

I suppose with the oil of the lemon we get some vitamin C and some mineral salts in our martini.

Some martini drinkers do not admit the twist of lemon. It is the olive or nothing.

In the film of *M*A*S*H* (1970), we see the young doctors, played by Elliott Gould and Donald Sutherland, in a field hospital tent just behind the lines in the Korean War.

Gould, who has just arrived, is offered a martini which is being served from IV drip-bags hanging in their mess, and he asks, 'Where are the olives?'

Sutherland replies, 'It's war — we have to make a concession.'

Gould says, 'Sorry, the martini just doesn't make it without the olive.'

This is a perfect illustration of the dogmas of martini folklore. It occurs to me that these martini dogmas and doctrines may also be a parody of religion. Or indeed, a fine substitute for religion.

Elliott Gould did not say what sort of olive he wanted but I suppose that as a drinker of classic martinis he would assume that there is only one acceptable olive for a martini. It is the green olive of whatever size cured in brine, never the black, although there is the cerignola olive which I have had in my martini and which is neither green nor black. It is a potato-shaped blue-grey and is not regular in shape and looks unusual in the martini glass, but I'm fond of this ungainly, fleshy olive; it has a certain jollity. There are about twenty species of olive but it is the age of the olive which determines its nature and size.

There is a very good bad joke from a *New Yorker* magazine cartoonist, J.B. Handelsman, about the olive and the twist.

The cartoon shows the bearded author Charles Dickens wearing a frockcoat in a New York bar. The caption reads: 'Dickens' First Encounter with a Martini'. In the cartoon, Dickens has just ordered his martini and the bartender is saying to him, 'Olive or twist?'

In the arcane world of the martini, one cannot ignore the ongoing complication of the olive *pip*.

Voltz and I discussed the olive pip in the Temple Bar, New York. I said, 'The dilemma is that with such an elegant drink as the martini the olive pip presents a "chewed bone" look when left in the glass or on a plate nearby or, worse, in an ashtray. No matter how much you work your teeth to get the olive flesh off the pip there will always be a rather inelegant-looking, ravaged pip.'

He agreed. 'If you put the chewed pips back into your glass they really disturb the elegance of the drink.'

I said that I knew that he and I usually put the pips in our pockets out of sight. 'The lemon twist never is a problem. It looks OK in the empty glass. Or it can be eaten.'

I told him that once in a dim restaurant Dr Anderson had put the olive pip in the salt dish. 'It was when they first started to put salt flakes in dishes on the table and took away the shakers.'

I told him that Dr Anderson had been seriously mortified. Voltz likes stories told against Dr Anderson, although they have never met.

Voltz said that given that men in trousers and jacket have up to twelve pockets available, why not use them? One pocket could be designated the olive pip pocket, say the left-hand jacket pocket. I sometimes fear that Voltz's pockets contain moulding olive pips from drinks past.

I told him that Australia had a Prime Minister, Malcolm Fraser, who, legend has it, would at cocktail parties or receptions put his olive pips in other people's pockets, which is a rather likeable if mischievous solution.

Voltz said, 'I like the sound of your Prime Minister but a roomful of people popping pips into each other's pockets seems undignified. Here in Manhattan you'll notice that no martini is ever garnished with an unpitted olive. They are garnished with olives stuffed with pimentos. I suppose they fear legal action from people who are drunk and break their teeth on the olive pip. I have no preference.'

I looked at him. It was almost unheard of for Voltz not to have a preference.

'The real problem,' he said, 'is that the unpitted olives are essential to a proper cocktail hour, in the martinis or not, just as hors d'oeuvres. And as we agreed, the pips are ugly when deposited with cigarette butts in an ashtray. And there are no ashtrays any more. What about using one of those little sake pitchers? If the olive pips aren't too large, we could drop them into the sake pitchers out of sight?'

I agreed that this could well be a solution. 'It would require some training of the guests. Guests can be beasts when it comes to training.'

'I have noticed that,' Voltz said. 'Guests are resistant to training.'

I told him that at my club in London, one of the initiation games is that the new members are served a martini with an unpitted olive in it and the committee then quietly watches what the newcomer does with the olive pip – whether he puts it on the table, back in the glass or in his pocket.

At the conclusion of the drink, the older members, without a word, then swallow their olive pips.

Voltz looked intently at my face while I told this story for evidence of fabulism. I didn't know whether he believed me. His face betrayed nothing and he did not interrogate me further.

The other practice is to place the pip in the folds of a napkin out of sight. While this is satisfactory it smacks a little of sweeping the dust under the carpet; the pips in the napkin become a dirty secret. (A second napkin should be requested if this is what you intend to do, for use in any of the possible emergencies which arise during the taking of a drink.)

Once when I met Voltz at Grand Central Oyster Bar, I could see that he was in a rage. 'In Elmore Leonard's book *Bandits* a character has a martini with three olives stuffed with anchovies – I frown on that,' he said.

I gave him my full attention while I ordered a pre-lunch martini. I could see he was ill-tempered.

'I frown on that because the anchovy is far too strong a flavour to introduce into the blend of a martini. It is an *assault* on the martini.'

'I agree,' I said, 'but perhaps Leonard is establishing the grossness of his character with this detail.'

'Novelists have to be very careful about these things, gross characters or not,' he said, taking his drink. 'To allow out into the world the very notion of an anchovy-stuffed olive in a martini, is to pollute the concept.'

'The epicurian M.K. Fisher fancies the anchovy-stuffed olive as an hors d'oeuvre.'

'We are not talking of hors d'oeuvres,' he said grumpily.

I tried to distract him from his rage. 'There is an almond stuffing but the nut looks alien in the olive already, let alone as an olive for a martini. It looks as if it lost its way from the nut dish.'

Voltz was undeterred. 'It has to be the capsicum stuffing or unpitted. Nothing else.'

I further tried to assuage him, by reminding him of Michael Swann, the songwriter, and his *Corrida d'Olivas* – or the Festival of Olive Stuffing. 'How many of you, I wonder, as you toy with a dry martini at the bar, have thought of the romance that lies behind the simple stuffed olive?' asks Swann. 'Or have witnessed, as I have, the almost unbearable drama of a *Corrida d'Olivas*?' He also claims that in Andora every boy hopes that he, too, will grow up to be one of the truly great *Oliveros*.

'I am pretty sure Swann made up that festival. I doubt that it exists,' Voltz said.

As I write this my mind goes back to my first taste of an olive. I was working as a journalist in a country town. The group I mixed with included Trevor, a gay solicitor, and his boyfriend, John. Paul had moved his work to the town so as to be with me. We were all very, very closeted.

This was before I married Margaret who was still back in the city. The four of us – Trevor and John, Paul and me – would sometimes eat at the best restaurant in the town called Romano's, which was in a hotel, as most restaurants in country towns were in those days.

It was Trevor who urged me to try green olives, which he ordered as an hors d'oeuvre to go with our pre-dinner drinks – gins and tonic, except for Paul who drank beer. The ordering of the olives was a fancy thing to do in those days, and we took our drinks in the upstairs lounge of the restaurant as distinct from the Public Bar or the Saloon Bar – for professionals and business-men – or the Ladies' Lounge where men had to be accompanied by a woman. The olives were the large green sort which we called a Spanish olive. As a nineteen-year-old of undeveloped tastes, I found them too bitter but each time we ate out, Trevor urged me to keep trying. 'They are an acquired taste,' he would say. It was the first time I had encountered the idea of an 'acquired taste' – and it was also my introduction to the aperitif and the hors d'oeuvre.

Trevor also introduced me to other important acquired tastes. He was to take – or be given – my anal virginity that year, and while taking male anal virginity is a unique pleasure, it is certainly an acquired taste.

I remember clearly going back one afternoon to his flat – John, his lover, was at work – and he *took me*, rather pleasantly. I remember saying to him, 'Well, I am no longer a virgin.'

For months I'd resisted his advances while still frequently going to visit him, flirtatiously, in his office. I lost my anal virginity to Trevor behind the back of Paul, who did not like anal sex and who, in turn, was my clandestine lover behind the back of my high-school girlfriend, Margaret, soon to be my wife.

There's infidelity for you.

Oh, and as for bisexuality, it's not as easy as it looks. Don't even think about it!

THE DIAMOND:
THE PEARL:
THE ACORN

NEW YORK (Reuters) – Drinkers might want to keep a clear head when ordering a martini at New York's historic Algonquin Hotel or they might pay $10,000 for that cold sip.

The landmark hotel, where famed wit Dorothy Parker and fellow literary lights at the Round Table imbibed, offers a $10,000 martini, complete with a loose diamond at the bottom.

Which reminds me of the legend of Cleopatra's (69 BCE) pearl drink.

There was something of a wager proposed by Cleopatra, Queen of Egypt, who had been defeated by Mark Antony and the

Roman armies. She bet Mark Antony she could put on a more expensive banquet than he could.

Mark Antony threw his banquet, which was magnificent beyond anything that had been seen in Egypt. He knew it would be impossible to spend any more than he had spent on wine and food.

Cleopatra then threw her banquet. After the feast, as Antony reclined eating his grapes, he did a quick calculation and decided that she had been unable to outdo him.

As the last course, Cleopatra called for two goblets of vinegar. Antony was bemused.

Cleopatra then took off one of a large pair of pearl earrings she was wearing – rumoured to be the most expensive piece of jewellery in history (worth 10 million sesterces if that means anything to you) – removed the pearl, and dropped it into the goblet, where it slowly dissolved. She then drank it.

She offered Antony the other pearl and the other goblet of vinegar.

Astonished, Antony declined the course – the matching pearl in the vinegar – and he and the other guests applauded her and acknowledged that she'd won. He later had the remaining pearl made into two earrings to replace the one she had dissolved and consumed.

'That,' I told Voltz in the Pen and Pencil one night, 'is said to be the most expensive drink in history.'

'How could she drink the vinegar?' Voltz asked, ever the sceptic. 'It'd be undrinkable.'

'A pearl is calcium carbonate, which can be dissolved in a weak acid solution such as vinegar, which is approximately 7%

acetic acid – formula: CH_3COOH.' Voltz loves it when I give him chemical formulas.

He nodded in approval. 'I knew you'd have a Wollongong answer.'

'The acidic vinegar is neutralised by the calcium carbonate of the pearl, much like an antacid tablet, so it becomes drinkable. Incidentally, some legends suggest that this drink is an aphrodisiac, probably conflated with the legends of oysters and virility. Don't try it at home.'

I didn't tell Voltz that it was more likely to have been a goblet of wine and that she probably swallowed the pearl and retrieved it the next morning. I did not think that the aesthetics of that would please him.

Strangely enough, my agent Rosemary Creswell then came in to the Pen and Pencil to join us and we linked up with a table of Americans, there in New York, who were, of all things, discussing the Australian early comic strip 'Ginger Meggs'. But that's another story.

My favourite animal martini cartoon from the *New Yorker* is that of a squirrel sitting quietly in a bar drinking a martini. Instead of an olive, he has an acorn in his martini.

Only squirrels are permitted to have acorns in their martinis. That's a universal rule.

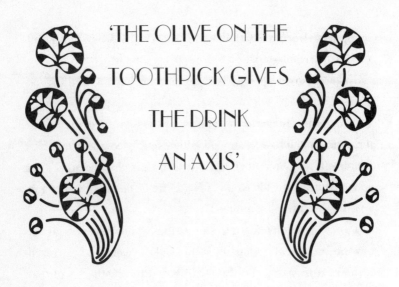

'THE OLIVE ON THE TOOTHPICK GIVES THE DRINK AN AXIS'

The girl in the Martini story in *Forty-Seventeen* observed that the toothpick gave the martini 'an axis'.

The martini does require a toothpick (sometimes called a cocktail stick but not by anyone I know) – but never one with a piece of coloured cellophane paper at one end and preferably one made from wood, although I have met people who prefer clear plastic toothpicks for no good reason. Voltz and I were told by a dentist martini drinker in Harry's Bar in Paris that plastic toothpicks are bad for the gums.

In Boston I usually eat at the traditional American restaurant Schroeders, or at the Union Oyster House with Sam Dettmann – the restaurant, by the way, which introduced the mass-produced toothpick to the US, at least that is what Sam told me over a martini in the Oyster House.

I guess I'm a wood snob, but I advise against tea-tree toothpicks (or chewing sticks as they are sometimes known) as being too strongly scented for the martini. The Maine white birch from which most US toothpicks are made is good.

Voltz told me in Mary's Bar that an American named Charles Forster invented the toothpick-making machine early in the 19th Century, but we know that the Americans and the Chinese are always claiming to have invented everything. Though the Chinese have not claimed the martini or the toothpick.

He continued, 'But I am having difficulty understanding how a toothpick comes from such large logs. I see many people filing down the logs to the size of a toothpick and I worry about the waste.'

I was able to tell him that the birch logs would be steamed to make them easier to work and then each log would be 'unwrapped' – its age layers separate and are peeled off into thin sheets; the flat toothpicks would be stamped out of these sheets, while I suppose round toothpicks would come from very tiny blocks which would be fed into a milling machine called a 'rounder' to make them circular.

'I am always appreciative of your technical knowhow.'

I said I preferred round to flat even if it meant more sawdust. I have a preference for those sharpened at only one end and I do like those with a small groove near the blunt end. I think these toothpicks look smarter. I don't like the ones that are pointed at both ends.

Voltz thought about this. 'I think the aesthetic question centres on the groove. Is it ornamental or does it have some purpose now lost to memory?'

'You mean a fairy or an elf, for example, could tie cotton around the toothpick and use it as, say, a harpoon?'

'I was not thinking along those lines. I don't often think about what fairies in their fairy economy might need or what use they might put a toothpick to.'

'There is nothing wrong with ornament.'

'The groove makes the toothpick a more serious-looking item,' he said. 'In my mind, that is. You can think fairy if you want.'

While I think it is OK to hold the toothpick in your mouth for a short time, as it seems to give some primal oral gratification, and I know some men seem to adopt it as a 'look', I want to say that I do not play bar games with toothpicks or matches. I will walk away when someone begins to arrange toothpicks or matches on the bar and I hear them saying something like, 'These twelve toothpicks represent six sheep pens of the same size. After one of the pieces of the fence is stolen, the farmer wants to rearrange the remaining pieces so that he will still have six pens of equal size. How does he do it?'

Another form of bar-room behaviour I find curious is the compulsion to tear things apart.

Voltz is a person who has a tendency to destroy his toothpicks. However, I am not going to discuss in any way – nor am I qualified to discuss – drinkers who are habitual twisters of cocktail straws, disintegrators of toothpicks, and shredders of cocktail napkins and coasters. Some of my other friends do these things. I ignore it when they do. Wreckers. Followers of Shiva, the Indian god of destruction. Though thankfully this tendency does not, in my experience, extend to the wrecking of bars or hotel rooms. As I look at their despairing messes, I wonder if it is a metaphor for their lives, a reflection of their inner selves. Sometimes I think, 'Out of the crooked timber of humanity no straight thing can ever be made.'

I say to them now, nothing is really a mess if you have words with which to analyse it accurately and to give it a verbal arrangement and an order.

Just for the record, I cannot see the point of using two toothpicks to suspend the olives across the glass from edge to edge *above* the martini, a practice which some bartenders feel is part of their contribution to the martini.

I once wrote about a rather eccentric character whose life ambition is to chair panel discussions at literary festivals.

The chairperson eventually ends up at a festival on Baffin Island. He reports that he 'will also be teaching the Eskimos the art of martini olive stick making, although timber is scarce on Baffin'. He continues:

Drinking martinis is what Eskimos call 'leaning into the wind', leaning into the wind, that is, of life.

Three things should be observed about the martini olive stick. It should be longer than the martini glass so that it can be twirled in a contemplative way while drinking and talking. The martini stick should have character as an object, and carry the dignity of the tree from whence it came . . . The stick should also impart the spirit of the forest to the drink which we know is there but which should not be discoverable in the blended taste of the whole drink. But yes, when the toothpick is in place in the martini, there resides in the drink the spirit of the forest.

Here on Baffin we talk a lot about the role of the martini and *quiviannikumut*. They are the same word in Eskimo and there is no easy translation, but roughly, it means 'to feel deeply happy while having total clarity about the wretched human condition'.

Ignorance suggests that there are no trees in the arctic. But under the snow there is a miniature forest of matted birches and willows. A sapling of a Richardson snow willow the thickness of a finger can contain two hundred years of growth rings. An Eskimo willow tree this old would yield about half a dozen martini sticks. Every two hundred years there would be wood for another six olive sticks.

It is worth pondering that my olive stick whittling demonstration will use up one thousand years of Eskimo forest. I acknowledge that as a craft industry it will be problematic for the Eskimo people and will conflict seriously with the principles of conservation.

Interestingly, the Eskimo word for forest translates as 'place of insufficient snow' and their word for 'picnic' means 'food shared with ants in place of insufficient snow'.

'The coldest martinis in the world are made on Baffin Island. As you know the problem with the martini is that people do not chill every ingredient sufficiently. On Baffin there is no trouble keeping everything chilled. Even the martini drinker's tongue is chilled.

Voltz and I have often talked about how the martinis would be in the famous hotel constructed of ice in Iceland. We both worry about the ambience of this ice hotel. Voltz is not willing to classify Reykjavík as a martini city.

'Perhaps the idea is more to be kept as a fantasy?' I suggested.

'We could do the figures on the idea of setting up a martini bar made of ice in Manhattan. As a business proposition.'

'The idea of a bar built of ice doesn't suggest the kind of contemplative lounging in a banquette that goes with the martini.'

'No. You're right. Don't bother doing the figures. Maybe we'll check out Reykjavík but I don't have high hopes.'

And before you say anything, I inquired of Sheila Rogers, a remarkable broadcaster at the Canadian Broadcasting Commission, and she told me that Innuits do not mind the word Eskimo. Eskimo is a strange word. The Oxford Dictionary says that it is Danish deriving from the French word *Esquimaux* (pl.), which in turn comes from the Algonquin language, and means, literally, 'eaters of raw flesh'. Australians invented the word 'esky' from Eskimo, to describe a portable insulated container, usually used for transporting drinks.

I once carved some toothpicks from a eucalyptus sapling and chose to believe that they added something to the martini. I sent half a dozen to Sheila Rogers, who raved about them.

The indefatigable Voltz reported another toothpick reference to me which is also admitted as a variation on the classic martini. 'I've been reading some hard-boiled 1950s fiction lately, and I found this in a book called *Wild Wives* by Charles Willeford.

'Willeford writes, "I call my martini a Desert Wind. Nine-tenths gin, one-tenth vermouth. No olive. No onion. Nothing. Just a toothpick."'

I find that a stark image — a clear martini with only a toothpick — a single leafless tree in a desert while the powerful wind of the martini blows around it.

As a side note, I have found that there is much social uneasiness about toothpicking. Voltz covers his mouth with his hand. Some people do it furtively with their fingernail when they feel they are unobserved. I think we should all be more open about it or, conversely, we should take a toothpick to the washroom after a meal and do it there.

It is the custom in civilised countries for restaurants always to place a container of toothpicks on the table during meals.

According to Elissa Schappell, an editor and contributor to *Tin House* magazine in NYC to which I also contribute, the writer Sherwood Anderson, *Winesburg, Ohio* (1919), died from peritonitis in 1941 after swallowing the toothpick while drinking a martini. I cannot imagine what it was that Anderson was doing with the toothpick, or the martini, or his mouth, or his hands which caused this to happen.

THEY HAD A DATE
WITH FATE IN
CASABLANCA

In film, in fiction and in folklore the martini cocktail has been a classy icon now for more than one hundred years. It is one of the great narratives of modern folklore. Dr Anderson and I would go on record as saying that the martini is also the most mentioned cocktail in English literature and in film.

These days, the martini is seen as a symbol of finer, older values – an embodiment of something lost, something worth reaching back for. It has come to represent a life of balance and taste – of connoisseurship.

The martini *glass*, in particular, has come to be the emblem of high times or swank times. The martini represents a signing-on for the pursuit of high times – the ordering of a martini is always an unspoken commitment.

Of all the cocktails – it is said that there are about six thousand listed cocktails (listed by whom? And where is this list? Voltz always asks) – it is the martini which has come to epitomise this quest for connoisseurship. For me, connoisseurship is an attitude of mind; it simply means being interested in knowing the fine things that the world has to offer and coming to know some of the discernments which our senses can convey (without becoming overly fastidious) while also knowing that we can never reach the end of this journey.

The fashionable or iconic beginnings of the martini coincide with the arrival of the cocktail hour in public places rather than in homes, and with the movie soundtrack in the late 1920s and along with this, the depiction of the cabaret and nightclub with all its talk, noises, music and possibilities.

The movie soundtrack allowed scriptwriters and film-makers to create the nightclub bar and cocktail-party style of fast conversation, wit, banter, repartee and smart talk – in the 1920s there was a magazine called *Smart Talk* – together with jazz, dance bands and blues and torch singers.

Perhaps since hearing this scripted clever-talk on the screen, we've had to speed up and smarten up our own conversation. And this cavorting on the screen probably spurred on the idea of creating the cocktail lounge at home where people were starting to have the makings of cocktails displayed on their sideboards and then in the cocktail cabinet or on the drinks' trolley.

One of my favourite martini scenes in movies (but not my favourite movie at all) is in *The Thin Man* (1934) in which Myrna Loy and William Powell play Nick and Nora, two upper-class private detectives created by Dashiell Hammett.

Powell is drinking in one of those great 1930s nightclub bars: Art Deco furnishing, bar stools, tables with table lamps (and sometimes table-to-table telephones), a black pianist playing jazz, tuxedos — almost the definition of a perfect martini bar until I heard Voltz arguing for the bar car on a moving train. Since Cambridge, we have discussed this idea further at Sardi's, and he has now amended his earlier dictum.

'I still think a train is the perfect place for a martini,' he said, 'but not all trains. Only trains travelling from or heading towards a martini city. I now think the train should be umbilically connected to a martini city. In *North by Northwest*, it was New York to Chicago — two martini cities. If you get on a train in Taos, New Mexico, bound for Salt Lake City, for example, you shouldn't have a martini.'

I argued that the train bar itself was a *place* in its own right and reminded him that we had decided that a train was, in fact, *an imperturbable space.*

'Maybe you're right,' he said. 'Maybe I worry too much about these matters.'

I reminded him that, anyhow, in *North by Northwest* Mr Thornhill (Cary Grant) drinks a Gibson.

'What has that got to do with anything? I was reminding you. You mustn't become pedantic,' he said.

'*I* mustn't become pedantic! That's rich.'

Probably to challenge his thinking somewhat, I then said that my London agent, Derek Johns, had named Istanbul as a martini city.

'On what grounds?' Voltz asked wearily. I told him Derek's story about Istanbul where his host mixed some martinis on the European shore of the Bosphorus, put them in an insulated container, and then he and Derek boarded a boat, sailed the short distance across the river to the Asian shore, where they drank their martinis. Derek said that it is the only city in which you can mix a martini on one continent and drink it on another.

Voltz refused to show that he was impressed by this story but said that he would 'take the Istanbul nomination under consideration'. He also worried that the insulated container would not have kept the martinis cold enough.

Anyhow, in *The Thin Man*, Nick (William Powell) has a martini in front of him when Nora (Myrna Loy) comes in. She is served a martini. She looks at Nick and realises that he is quite drunk and asks, 'How many martinis have you had?'

He says six.

Nora calls to the barman, 'All right, will you bring me five more martinis, Leo? And line them up right here.'

If, as Voltz argues, glasses were smaller in the 1930s, Nora's drinking of six martinis makes more sense. Or were the drinks weaker? Or the human bodies stronger? Or the appetite for life stronger? Six martinis by today's measure is a lot of martinis.

But the point is that this scene is a stunning assertion of the social mobility of the New Woman and the uni-sexual nature of the martini.

Nora as played by Myrna Loy shows that in 1934 she can enter the bar without a man.

She can talk directly to the barman.

And she can order her own drink.

She can even go to excess.

She can ask for, and get, what she wants.

What was reflected in films was being played out in real life. It was in the nightclub and the lounges of grand hotels that women crossed another historic line in social mobility. The drink that symbolised this moment in history was the martini. It was also the time for wearing make-up during the day and the invention by Helena Rubenstein in Paris in 1921 of the handbag compact mirror and the lipstick tube. Men began to see women checking, and even refreshing, their make-up at the bar.

It really began with the arrival of the fashionable department store in the second half of the 19th Century. Women could, for the first time, go into the city alone or with other women to shop at these stores, or for morning or afternoon tea or lunch in the store dining room unchaperoned and unaccompanied by a man and unobserved by the 'village'.

It was not too far down the block from the department store tearooms to the lounges of grand hotels and then to the cocktail lounge or a fashionable restaurant where respectable women could, for the first time, drink in public without men. And then not too far to the nightclub and all it promised.

Most would agree the most famous nightclub in film history is Rick's Café Américain in *Casablanca*. The story is set almost entirely in a 1940s nightclub, Rick's, run by Humphrey Bogart, in Morocco. To quote the Hollywood publicity tagline for the film: 'They had a date with fate in Casablanca!'

For me, the nightclubs of those times were characterised by chance meetings and introductions. In Rick's we have conspiratorial meetings, accidental reunions, life-changing introductions, arrests by the police, deals done, fates decided, money won and lost and falling in love – the most dramatic of all chance meetings. Sadly, no martinis are drunk in *Casablanca*.

To illustrate how acceptable public drinking of cocktails had become at this time, I quote from Mary McCarthy's book *The Group*, set in 1930s America. McCarthy describes a scene in a hospital where a friend is sick: '. . . it was cocktail hour in Priss's room at New York Hospital – terribly gay . . . Sloan dropped in every afternoon and shook up martinis for visitors . . . Mrs Hartshorn swallowed her martini in a single draft, like medicine: this was the style among advanced society women of her age . . . she refused a "dividend" from the silver shaker . . .'

The American drinking expression the dividend refers to the second or remaining part of a martini in the coctail shaker, which is usually watered down a little by the melting ice.

When Voltz and I were drinking a martini in the bar of the Downtown Association Club in Manhattan, of which I am a reciprocal member, the martinis were served in small individual jugs containing more than a full martini from which the waiter initially filled our glasses at our table. When we had finished our first martini, the waiter came over and asked us if we would 'like the dividend'. We, of course, said yes, and he poured what was left in the jugs into our glasses – not quite a full second martini.

The cocktail hour, the pre-dinner drink – the civilised idea of ending the day with friends or family (if you can find either) and a drink; perhaps better described as 'starting the night' – seems to have begun in 16th Century Europe (who knows?) when people produced spirits flavoured with herbs and spices for medicinal purposes which included the stimulation of appetite (any old excuse). What was so wrong with their appetites in the 16th Century? I'm willing to bet that at some point – say, immediately? – the medicinal purpose was thoroughly abused or at least stretched. But every time I have a Campari, more than in any other drink, I taste 16th Century. I taste its medicine. And I take its medicine. The aperitif is a drink to stimulate the appetite but how it is supposed to do this has never been adequately explained to me. Perhaps it relaxes the stomach and the spirits after the stress of the day, or maybe it introduces some gentle enzymes into the stomach.

The early producers of the 'medicinal' aperitif made it more acceptable to the taste by diluting the ingredients in wine, vermouth being one of these. In France it is known as the *apero* and takes place usually at 7 pm, after the *cinq-à-sept*, the French expression for an afternoon meeting between lovers (what is sometimes known as the martini matinée). I don't know whether any alcohol that afternoon lovers drink is considered an *apero*. In Italy it is called the *aperitivo* – both words come from the Latin word *aperire*, 'to open', as in open the bar.

Somewhere in the 1920s the martini became the prince of *aperitifs*.

The traditional French aperitifs are port and pastis and the Italian are vermouth or Campari. (Campari is a bitter Italian aperitif made of a blend of herbs and alcohol developed in 1860 by Sig. Gaspare Campari in Milan.) The English seem to begin earlier with Scotch, gin drinks, and Pimms. There is the American Happy Hour. I have had to point out to bartenders in the two-for-the-price-of-one Happy Hour bars that two martinis cannot acceptably be served to one person at the same time. The second martini will, of course, lose its chill and the queueing of drinks in front of one at a bar intimates excess of the lesser order. If there are two people, there is obviously no problem.

Voltz is adamant that in Manhattan when he was growing up, the cocktail hour began with the nightly news. One fetched a drink from the cocktail tray – his family did not have a trolley – and then went in to listen to the news. 'You would take a drink so as to face and digest the news. I suppose it makes doing your civic duty more pleasant.'

He agreed that this rule only applied if you found yourself in the unfortunate position of being at home at the cocktail hour.

Quite early in my life I developed a taste for stylish bars and clubs away from the egalitarian public bar.

You cannot confidently order a martini in a public bar. That is asking too much of a public bar.

My friend the late Murray Sime, a lawyer and a senior vice president of Citigroup, always preferred the pub. He felt that there was a greater chance of meeting the unexpected in a pub. And he usually did.

Sometimes he quoted G.K. Chesterton, usually missing a line or two and rewriting others (and God knows where he dredged it up from).

. . . It is not true to say I frowned,
Or ran about the room and roared;
I might have simply sat and snored
I rose politely in the club
And said, 'I feel a little bored.
Will someone take me to a pub?'

I do like a bar where I am likely to bump into old friends or acquaintances. I sometimes prefer the chance meeting to the arranged meeting and there are some people I prefer to meet by chance. I suppose that is what a warm acquaintance is.

Oh, I nearly forgot. The cocktail hour can be longer than an hour.

LIBERATING
THE RITZ

In 1944 Hemingway was covering the war in France for *Colliers* magazine. He heard that the Germans were retreating from Paris, so he armed himself with a Sten gun – a British lightweight sub-machine gun from S and T, the initials of the inventors' surnames, Shepherd and Turpin – gathered together some ten French 'irregulars', and joined up with an American OSS (espionage) officer, Colonel David Bruce, who himself had about thirty men and some stray soldiers.

They set off into Paris, which was being liberated from the German army by American soldiers and French Resistance.

There was still some sniper fire, but most of the German soldiers had retreated.

Hemingway led the group to the Ritz Hotel, where he and Bruce had stayed before the war. The Germans who had been using the hotel as a base had fled and it was empty.

The manager of the hotel, M. Ausiello, recognised them and greeted them. M. Ausiello said to Hemingway, 'Can I get you anything?'

Hemingway looked behind him at the men gathered there, and said, 'How about seventy-three dry martinis?'

The manager and barman lined them up on the bar, and the group of soldiers and irregulars drank to the 'liberation of the Ritz'.

There is no record of the proportions or ingredients of the martinis.

Hemingway took two prisoners, a couple of elderly German orderlies who had been left behind doing the laundry.

The Ritz commemorated this event by naming the bar Bar Hemingway. But when I was in Paris for the opening of the new Ritz bar last year along with Voltz and the usual riff and raff, I found there is some controversy about all this. There is the bar in which Hemingway drank as a regular – the Ritz bar – and the Bar Hemingway, which was the bar he 'liberated' on that day in 1944.

Voltz argues that to *sense* Hemingway, it is best to drink in the Ritz bar, despite the memorabilia in the Bar Hemingway.

I argue that the Ritz bar has been so extensively renovated that it is not really the same bar where Hemingway drank, and that it is difficult to sense Hemingway there now.

Voltz says, 'And another thing. Did they drink the martinis *as they were made* or wait for all of them to be made before drinking them? If they waited, wouldn't the seventy-three martinis have all been at vastly varied temperatures?'

I prefer not to discuss this with Voltz.

THE FIRST
MARTINI FILM

In 1928 there was a silent comedy made called *Dry Martini* directed by a person with the unlikely name of Harry d'Abbadie d'Arrast. It is based on a book by John Thomas entitled *Dry Martini: A Gentleman Turns to Love* (1926).

A film historian says that d'Arrast directed films that were acclaimed for their wit, sophistication and smooth pacing, those things we associate with the martini, but the film *Dry Martini*, along with that first fashionable martini-drinking generation of the 1920s, is considered by archivists to be 'lost'.

Legend has it that d'Arrast gave up movies to live off the roulette tables of Monte Carlo. Martini-drinking can lead to that sort of existence.

The book's story is simple. The twenty-one-year-old daughter of a decadent American father who is living in Paris, turns up to visit her long-absent father, the legendary bon vivant, hoping to be taught decadence. The decadent father, not realising that this is what his daughter wants, sets out to teach her 'respectability' and puts on an act as a proper parent while she, disappointed by her now seemingly respectable father, has to set out to find decadence by herself.

I sent Thomas's book to Voltz for his birthday.

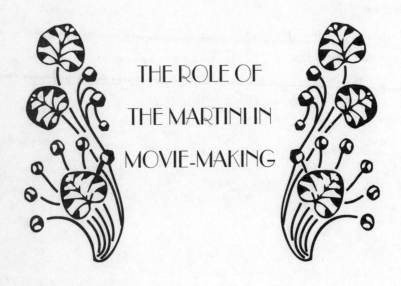

THE ROLE OF
THE MARTINI IN
MOVIE-MAKING

The last slate of the day on a movie set is sometimes called 'the martini'.

A MARTINI
MATINÉE

August Kleinzahler, in 'Diary', in the *London Review of Books*, 4 November 2004, has this note on the poet Thom Gunn: 'Thom [Gunn] remembered him [Auden] going on at some length about martinis, what constituted a good one and where the best were to be found. This subject would have been of little or no interest to Thom then.

'Although we were good friends for 23 years, our friendship reached its apotheosis ['Does he mean "apogee"?' Dr Anderson asked as we drank a martini in the Royal Automobile Club and examined this note by Kleinzahler] over the last few years of Thom's life, after his retirement from teaching, in our martini matinées. The word matinée has an old-fashioned, low meaning as an "afternoon tryst", but our martini matinées were only that: martinis at both ends of an afternoon movie.'

A few years earlier, in my black academic gown, I had gone to Thom Gunn's memorial service at King's College, Cambridge.

'... THE ORCHESTRA IS PLAYING YELLOW COCKTAIL MUSIC ...'

The cocktail hour also invites music and I love the piano bar, blues bars, and jazz bars. There is a genre of music called Lounge which is acceptable.

Murray Sime and I would often have crustless, quarter-cut lobster sandwiches at the old Menzies Hotel with our martinis while listening to the harpist.

Voltz usually says, 'No music is good too.'

Yes, no music is good too.

'Better none, than bad.'

Agreed.

Scott Fitzgerald wrote, 'The lights grow brighter as the earth lurches away from the sun, and now the orchestra is playing yellow cocktail music . . . one of the Gypsies seizes a cocktail out of the air . . .'

My Birth Song (the song that was top of the hit parade on the day I was born – an idea dreamed up by Ian Van Tuyl) is 'Moonlight Cocktail' sung by Glenn Miller.

>Couple of jiggers of moonlight and add a star,
>Pour in the blue of a June night and one guitar,
>Mix in a couple of dreamers and there you are:
>Lovers hail the Moonlight Cocktail . . . dah dah dah . . .
>Follow the simple directions and they will bring
>Life of another complexion where you'll be king.

Not true.

CANAPÉS

At the cocktail hour, I love canapés and other hors d'oeuvres or what is now rather baldly called 'bar food'. Hors d'oeuvres means literally 'outside the main work', outside the main meal.

Nuts are fine but should be eaten only once a month otherwise they become habitual and eaten without appreciation; likewise potato crisps — perhaps once every two months for potato crisps. Nuts and crisps must never be eaten from the packet but always put into dishes. It is not acceptable to fashion a crisp or nut packet into a dish shape, though in rougher bars it is sometimes inescapable. Knowledge of origami can be handy here.

Actually, you should never drink a martini in a bar that does not serve its nuts or crisps in bowls.

And never take *handfuls* — voracious grasps — of nuts from a bowl. Voltz says that it is OK to take a handful as long as you don't put it in your mouth in one go. I disagree. No handfuls.

The practice of *prana* (eating slowly and concentrating on what it is you are eating, at least momentarily and from time to time) requires that you eat each nut singularly and savour it. Taking one nut at a time from the bowl should be sufficient. If you are hungry, order a canapé.

I expounded to Voltz in the Yale Club Bar that as we eat our one peanut at a time, we should always spare a thought for the great distance it has travelled, and how it has been cared for by many hands: those that prepared the soil of the field in which it grew, those who planted the seeds of that peanut, the hands that irrigated it and cared for the growing plants, the hands that picked the peanut, the packers who put them in boxes, and the hands of the people who put them into packets as they came down the assembly line, the person who designed the packet, the people who manufactured the packet, the labellers of the packet, the truck loaders, the ship loaders, the waterside workers, the wholesalers who carefully stored the peanuts, the delivery people who carried the nuts to your particular bar, the shop assistants who arranged the packages on shelves, the food inspectors.

'Isn't this headed towards the finicky?' Voltz asked.

As if Voltz would know where the boundary lies between finicky and plain living.

'We can't be too finicky, I think, about these matters. It's a question of deliberation.'

Voltz grasped my arm and looked me in the eye. 'You're damned right. We can't be too finicky in this shithouse world.'

Voltz is fond of saying that the world is going to hell in a handcart.

Of course, if you are pigging out, anything goes. I have pigged out. Go ahead, eat the whole bowl of nuts in two handfuls and drink the martini straight down and think nothing of the long line of people who brought these gifts to your mouth. But not every time.

The epicurian M.K. Fisher suggests '. . . generous, rich, salty Italian hors d'oeuvres: prosciutto, little chilled marinated shrimps, olives stuffed with anchovy, spice and pickled tomatoes . . .'

And of course the Spanish have tapas.

The hors d'oeuvres at the Bayswater Brasserie are, I consider, among the best I have ever found anywhere in the world, though some of the offerings are perhaps a little too robust for the cocktail hour.

– foie gras served with toast (foie gras is, of course, best eaten with Sauterne)
– oysters freshly shucked or in tempura (though I would never drink a martini with an oyster – a flinty dry Riesling or Sancerre or Chablis, Champagne or beer would be best with oysters)
– chickpea and flat bread (Turkish bread)
– salt and pepper squid
– prawn and pork gyoza
– salmon fish cakes
– mixed cheese and fruit and lavosh (though cheese for me still belongs after the main course – but go ahead, have it, I won't say anything)

– hot potato chips with homemade chilli and tomato ketchup.

It is a pity they do not offer canapés. A canapé is somewhat smaller – bite size – and is created on a platform of bread; it is, after all, the French word for sofa – the toppings sit on the sofa of bread.

The canapé is usually about a centimetre thick, and can be shaped with a cutter into circles, oblongs, squares, triangles or other fancy shapes.

These portions of bread are sautéed in butter or used as bases for fresh combinations of lettuce, egg, ham, sardine, anchovy, lobster, crab, oyster.

I recently came across a recipe for the oyster sandwich from the early 20th Century: 'Arrange fried oysters on crisp lettuce leaves, allowing two oysters for each leaf, and one leaf for each sandwich. Prepare as other sandwiches.'

As a copyboy on the old *Daily Telegraph* it was one of my nightly jobs to go to a nearby restaurant and collect oyster sandwiches for the owner of the paper, Frank Packer, Kerry's father. The oysters were out of a bottle and the sandwiches were made from white bread and butter.

I sometimes eat an oyster sandwich but my oysters are freshly shucked.

Sandwiches at cocktails should be crustless and cut into small triangles – or what my club calls a 'six point'.

In the country town where I grew up my mother would serve cubed cheddar cheese and coloured pickled onions on tooth-picks, which were displayed on holders made for displaying these delicacies. One of the holders she had was a small horse which I fancied. As a child I also enjoyed the leftovers from her afternoon parties. I suspect that is where I got my taste for hors d'oeuvres and, by extension, cocktails.

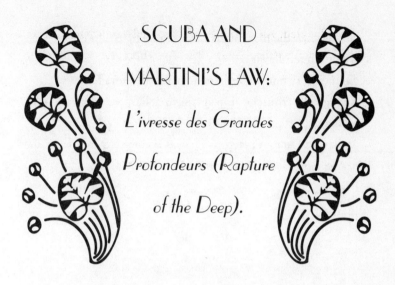

SCUBA AND MARTINI'S LAW:

L'ivresse des Grandes Profondeurs (Rapture of the Deep).

In the Leda Bar on the cruise ship *Orion* while in the Torres Strait, the biologist Len Zell told me about the international scuba-diving rule known as Martini's Law.

He quoted Jacques Cousteau in *The Silent World*: 'I am personally quite receptive to nitrogen rapture. I like it and fear it like doom – *L'ivresse des Grandes Profondeurs* has one salient advantage over alcohol: no hangover. If one is able to escape from its zone, the brain clears instantly and there are no horrors in the morning. I cannot read accounts of a record dive without wanting to ask the champion how drunk he was.'

Len says that nitrogen acts as an anaesthetic which can have an intoxicating effect. Martini's Law states that every fifteen metres of diving is equal to the effect of one martini. Divers experience 'a feeling of stimulation, excitement and euphoria, occasionally accompanied by laughter and loquacity'.

Sometimes the diver does not wish to return to the surface and sometimes doesn't.

Sounds very much like some martini drinkers I know.

I rang Voltz from the ship at twelve dollars a minute and told him this important information.

Voltz said, 'At four martinis I feel as if I am sixty metres below life. And I aways wish to stay there.'

MADEMOISELLE
AND THE
DOCTOR AND
THE MARTINI

I saw a documentary (*Mademoiselle and The Doctor* made by Janine Hosking, 2005) about an eighty-year-old French woman, Lisette Nigot, who planned to suicide at eighty because she felt her life was completed; she had no reason to get up in the morning. She denied loneliness or ill health and spoke with good humour as she explained her intentions.

She talked to a doctor about the final alcoholic drink she would have with her suicide drugs and said she had chosen vodka with fruit juice because it would make the drugs she was to use more palatable.

But, she said, gin was her favourite drink and then her face was lit with a very special kind of smile filled with memories and connection and she said, 'Best of all I like a dry martini.' It was a love of the life attitude that the martini suggested to her. She felt that the martini would be spoiled if mixed with the drugs.

Shortly after this interview she did suicide.

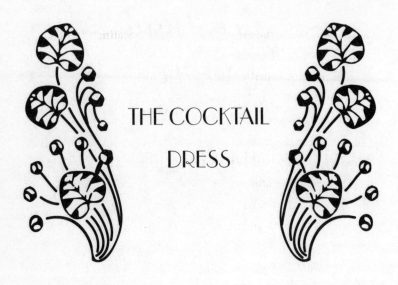

THE COCKTAIL
DRESS

It's OK to wear your cocktail dress – the little black dress or a sheath dress – on to dinner after the cocktail hour. No need to change.

The cocktail dress should be made from one of the lightweight sensual fabrics – satin, silk, velvet – and can be embroidered and trimmed. Underwear should harmonise. We wear our newer, more sexy underwear and we use our Other Perfume and change our jewellery to the more precious or least worn.

Women's evening clothing especially is designed to make 'windows to the body'. According to fashion, it can be the breast cleavage, the legs revealed as high as you wish, shoulders, the back as low as you dare, the hint of buttock cleavage, and arms and armpits revealed according to taste. The ankle as a point of revelation has been lost to us as the hemline of dresses has permanently risen, although I can imagine a return to ankle-length skirts and dresses — the Muslim Look? I am doubtful about the exposed belly and navel at cocktails. There is a certain beach casualness to this look. Voltz agrees.

I could make an exception about the exposed belly if the dress was made by Geoffrey Beene. In the autumn of 1996 in New York, he made an evening gown from silver panne velvet, which if I remember it correctly, had 'breast plates', two silver rectangles joined at the neck, then parting and spreading over the breasts. Silver cord secured the material under the breasts, crossed at the back and then at the exposed navel. The back too was bare to the cleavage of the buttocks, except for thin silver straps coming from the neck crossing mid-back and then continuing around to the front to connect to the breast plates.

Men should change into a tux (worn originally at the Tuxedo Club in New York during the late 19th Century and copied from a similar male jacket being worn at the time in Europe). In the UK it is known as 'black tie', and the French call it a 'smoking'. The tux can be worn after six pm. The word *tuxedo* seems to be an Algonquin word for the land around where Tuxedo Park now is.

Voltz and I favour silk lapels.

THE WHOLE
QUESTION OF THE
DRINKS' CART

There is the public or club cocktail bar and there is drinking at home. The biggest argument Voltz and I have had is over the question of the drinks' cart (or as I prefer, 'trolley').

It happened this way.

'Stainless steel cocktail shakers are to be preferred,' Voltz stated, 'because they get much colder than glass, but it's also a style question. Steel shakers evoke dining cars and Art Deco penthouses. Maybe the ideal is the bullet-shaped shaker from the 1930s, which would hold about five martinis with ice and has an internal strainer. I also accept glass pitchers – blown glass, not cut glass – which evoke the drinks' cart.'

I told Voltz that in the early 1930s, especially in the year after Prohibition ended, the cocktail shaker became the most popular Christmas gift in the US, but I then felt compelled to add, 'While I am relieved by your remarks about blown glass and the stainless steel shaker – I agree about the achieved coldness of the stainless steel and the bullet-shaped shaker, although I would personally prefer a dial-a-drink cocktail shaker where you can find the recipe of different great 1920s cocktails such as a Gin Ricky or Side Car by turning the barrel of the shaker to the desired drink – I am, however, unsettled by your reference to a drinks' cart. A tray, yes, a butler's table, yes, but a drinks' *cart*?!'

I told him that when I was growing up my family used what was called a traymobile – known in some places as an autotray – a small double-level table, on casters, in my home used for serving tea at every meal, but which could have been used for serving drinks had drinks ever been served in my home. My mother always served the tea. One model that I've seen has a tray with handles inset as the top shelf which can be removed by its handles when the traymobile has arrived at its destination.

I said that for the serving of the martini, it was my opinion that the plain, round, metal bar tray is surely enough (a tray, along with the cup, is another artefact sculpted from the outstretched human hands – the two human hands were the first tray). The tray should not carry advertising, especially not antique advertising.

I explained to Voltz that the problem with the drinks' cart was that it somehow *over-elaborated* the presentation of the martini. The drinks' cart usually over time comes to be a display of expensive and exotic drinks and also gathers drinking gadgets and bar novelties.

'I enjoy the display of all the liquors and beers but only in a public cocktail bar as an illustration of choice and abundance and colour and shape and possibility; as a matter of fact, I think this backlit display is the glory of the good bar and it is sometimes a delight to be, as the American poet John Berryman says, "lost in the forest of bottles".

'But at home the martini must be granted its place as a pedigree drink. It detracts from the dignified simplicity of the martini to serve the martini from an array of miscellaneous bottles on a drinks' trolley, that is, presenting it as just another drink among many. The martini needs a clear stage. That's all I'm saying.'

In the Algonquin bar one night I returned to the question of the drinks' cart and told Voltz that designers refer to the drinks' cart as 'an accent piece', that is, a distinctive feature of the room, something that calls attention to itself. 'Which is also a black mark against it. I am not wanting to be difficult about all this but it seems that we resolve the matter of the metal shaker and the glass pitcher only to be disturbed by another issue – the cart.'

Voltz replied patiently, 'The proper drinkers' drinks' cart is never for show and never stocked with fancy liquors. The owner of a proper drinks' cart is an aesthetically serious person and has no time – nor, especially, space – to waste on frivolous gadgets and undrunk exotic gift bottles.

'A drinks' cart usually contains the drinker's libation and the glasses that match it and that's all. For instance, straight bourbon drinkers would never bother with highball glasses on their drinks' cart.

'If I recall correctly, all James Stewart's lovelorn artist pal had on her drinks' cart in *Vertigo* was a bottle of Scotch and a few cafeteria-style water glasses. That is correct style.

'A drinks' cart would sit in your office or living room, preferably under a window. On the bottom shelf of the cart would be a silver ice bucket, engraved with your initials, which can be carried to the fridge, filled with ice, and then returned to the top shelf of the drinks' cart where there would always be room for it. Even if ice is not required it should be there.

'There would be a glass pitcher with a long brass spoon. And there would be the bottom half of a steel martini shaker, its top long lost.'

He went on to say that the cocktail cabinet was another matter. 'It is the cocktail cabinet which is the domain of the pointless, showy and silly, along with these "dens" or "rathskellers" that men often create. They're more like altars to a style of masculinity – they belong to another aesthetic and to a certain dumb "novelty" humour. They contain gift liquors, liquors in funny bottles – in the shape, say, of a guitar – liquors stolen from airplanes, liquors from exotic countries and in odd colours. Themes are common: gambling, golf, fishing and horse racing imagery often appear printed on novelty glasses. Also, there may be an ashtray from Florida with a sailfish on it and there may be a table lamp in the shape of a streetlamp with a drunk leaning up against it that sings "How Dry I Am" when switched on.'

I said to Voltz, 'I know what you mean by the den bar. But to return to your description of your model drinks' cart, it concerns me still. I see in my mind those faux wheels on the cart which worry me. In fact, it is the pointless wheels which worry me most. Surely the drinks' cart, if it is a cart, should be truly mobile in the same way that a wheelbarrow or traymobile is mobile. Not fraudulently mobile. The wheels on drinks' carts these days are no longer just castors, the wheels now are large, silly imitation wheels sometimes with spokes, imitating wagon wheels. And, anyhow, you can't get a drinks' cart up and down stairs or steps, wheels or no wheels. If it isn't mobile then it shouldn't have wheels. The wheels contravene the principles of functional modernism, surely?'

I also raised the drinks' cart question with my friend Matt and told him of Voltz's vexing position. He said, 'John Birmingham has such a cart in his loungeroom over at Bondi, twin-shelfed with, if memory serves, four wheels. From my observations, the cart has never been moved, thus bringing into question your point about the purpose of wheels and the functionality of the cart itself.

'His cart has stainless steel framing and mirrored shelves. This would suggest that somewhere along the line this range of cart was manufactured with the "mobile cocktail cabinet" idea in mind, a focal point in the room, a little window, if you like, for grander aspirations and sophisticated yearnings — what you would call an "accent piece".

'I might add my father had one of Voltz's den-style bars in the 70s, and the sign behind it read "I allus has one at eleven".

'In its favour, it has to be said that at least the drinks' trolley announces to the world that we like a bit of a tipple and we're perfectly happy for that notion to be asserted in our home furnishings.'

I told Matt that his observations about the drinks' trolley and aspirations and it being an 'announcement' were very pertinent. I told him that in the Victorian period in England the sideboard became such an announcement in many homes although before that the aristocracy used opulent sideboards for display sometimes including a built-in wine cooler. It was a small stage upon which the householder's silver was displayed and upon which expensive dishes were served.

I passed Matt's considerations on to Voltz, again expressing my concern about the useless wheels on the cart. Voltz replied, 'Need I remind you of why there are buttons on the sleeve of your jacket? Frederick the Great put them there to discourage his men from wiping their noses on their sleeves while on parade. In the same way, the wheels of the drinks' cart have no "memory" of the reason they were put there. Wheels are not an issue.'

I said that I failed to see how three or four buttons would stop a determined soldier on parade from wiping his nose on his sleeve. 'You just wipe it on the other side of the jacket – try it.'

Voltz came back and said, 'That is not my point.'

I was determined to resolve this dispute and investigate the origins of the drinks' trolley.

Through the Victoria and Albert Museum in London, I was able to track down one of the designers of the original 1930s drinks' trolleys, the Hungarian designer Susan Kozma, now in her nineties. She designed the famous Kozma drinks' trolley, one of the first. Her Kozma drinks' trolley is now on display in the V and A.

I explained to her my worries about the wheels and Voltz's lack of concern.

'You and your friend Voltz are both wrong about the wheels,' she said. 'But you are the more wrong. When I designed my drinks' trolley for the Schreibers in Budapest in 1938 it was part of the living-room furniture which I designed for them.

'The living room had a divan, chairs, and this drinks' trolley and a number of built-in pieces of furniture. In keeping with modernist principles of the times, that which was not built-in was made to be easily moved, so the room was open and flexible – you could rearrange the room easily according to what was happening in it that day. If the room was to be used for cocktails you could move furniture to make an appropriate space and so on. Do you follow me?' she said, sternly.

Susan Kozma's drinks' trolley from 1938 is a stylish, large box on wheels with a chrome handlebar for pushing it. Nothing of its contents were displayed. When opened, two half-sections of the box swung out on hinges to reveal shelves and bottles and glasses – in fact, it was a mobile cocktail cabinet.

I was chastened by Susan Kozma's judgement. However, it is my experience that rooms once arranged tend to stay arranged, although I did not have the courage to say this to her. Years go by and very little is ever changed. People may refurbish once or twice in a lifetime. They rarely change their wall paintings. People seem to like things to stay the way they are although, sadly, it means over time they no longer see their rooms.

One of the nice results of Miss Kozma's rebuke was that I came to see that while the wheels on the drinks' cart very quickly lose their memory, the forgotten wheels may dream – I like to think that now they sit there dreaming of when they were both mobile and chic in the fashionable rooms of pre-war Budapest, Paris and Berlin.

Recently, Voltz wrote, saying, 'I recalled your defence of the simple drinks' tray last week when I attended Noël Coward's *Private Lives* on Broadway as the guest of a Hollywood bigwig I know. Afterwards, we had drinks in Alan Rickman's dressing room with the cast and a few of his friends. It was very Noël Cowardish and I espied a martini shaker on a drinks' tray (just a tray, alas) with glasses on it sitting by his dressing table. I complimented him on the appropriateness of having a martini shaker in his dressing room during a Noël Coward production, but he dismissed it with a shrug and said it was a gift. He served white wine.

'We had martinis afterwards in oakey bars on the Upper East Side. There's still civilisation in this rotten world.'

Again, a few months after the controversy of the drinks' cart, Voltz said to me in the bar of the White Horse, 'I was watching a Fred Astaire movie last night, *The Pleasure of His Company* – only worth watching for the 1960s furnishings. Especially of interest: a top-opening drinks' *cabinet*, as distinct from the cupboard-style cocktail cabinet. It resembled a stereo cabinet: the lid opens up (there may be a mirror on the underside of it, there may be utensils clipped there) and you have to reach inside to get the bottles and glasses. A nice alternative to the drinks' cart with the advantage that its contents are not displayed. In that way, it resembles the 1938 drinks' trolley. And, by the way, in the script of *The Big Sleep*: "Norris enters, pushing a teawagon bearing decanter, siphon, initialled ice bucket".

'You are right about that, at least; evidently in the 1940s a bar cart was an adapted teawagon. Your mother used the traymobile correctly.'

One of the things I like about Voltz is that he never gives up.

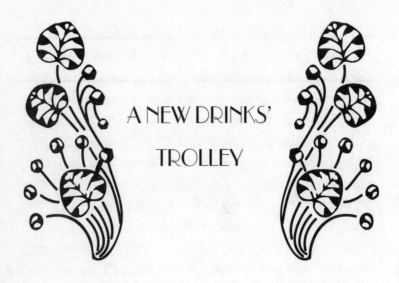

A NEW DRINKS' TROLLEY

'Dear Matt, Today I purchased my first drinks' trolley and have equipped it pretty much to your specifications. It is stainless steel and frosted glass, two shelves with a wine rack at the bottom, for, say, six bottles — I never have had more than six bottles in my life at any given time. It has a handle to push it. It is where Art Nouveau meets Art Deco, geometry meets organic image: that is, the sides of the trolley are three bands of three curving parallel metal rods equally spaced. It is on casters.

'I push it around my apartment although I have yet to "entertain" anyone with it. At present it has a bottle of half-drunk Shiraz, a full bottle of JD, a measuring cup given to me by my three best graduate students from Texas (who in God's name measures drinks?), a bottle of orange bitters from you, and a champagne resealer (who ever needs to reseal champagne?).'

Matt replied, 'On the purchase of a trolley: have you purchased the trolley for the aesthetics of the trolley itself or is it a "nesting" urge you may now be experiencing? Having purchased the trolley, it now must have a home. You have committed the trolley to your environment which is now the trolley's "turf".

'Although I know you have a few select pieces of fine furniture in your life, which orbit you like moons, and perhaps the trolley has now been installed in that firmament. Nevertheless, by virtue of purchase it has now become a part of the texture that is you. Are you prepared for this?

'On the pushing around of the trolley in the absence of guests: I think this is entirely legitimate and in some way sends a line across time and space back to the yum cha maids and perhaps a deep desire you have to serve, to present goods and bounty and beautiful things to other people. Which, naturally, is one of the functions of writing.

'Perhaps we push drinks' trolleys all our lives in order to please and illuminate. Solo trolley pushing in the privacy of one's home is surely a way of revelling in the craft and refreshing what is so intrinsic to us, a secret celebration.

'On what is presented on the trolley: Allow me to go out on a limb and suggest the trolley has its own "ID". Even as the craftsmen were making the trolley and assembling the chrome and checking the casters, what would go on that trolley immediately and decades into the future was already established at that moment of creation. To establish what works on the trolley you only have to look at you, what pleases you both in terms of taste and drinking habit, but what functions for you, primarily, on a day-to-day basis.

'The martini, for you, is the maypole of your trolley. The second, bourbon. The rest — champagne, bitters, wine — or all those other things that please guests, are secondary, and the trolley should only be burdened temporarily with them to coincide with entertaining other than one's self.

'The trolley can be "dressed up" for these moments, just as we dress up for specific occasions, but at all other times surely it must revert to its pared back "ID".

'On losing the aesthetics of the trolley to knick-knacks: I don't want to sound harsh but I think the champagne resealer and the measuring cup are a mistake that you may later regret. The champagne resealer is not only offensive and the tit on a bull of the myriad little knick-knacks that the drinking industry has literally thrown up for people of dubious taste and with "home bars". It is an insult to the people being served the champagne. It says unspeakable things about a person willing to put the resealer into the open bottle and return it to a refrigerator.

'The bourbon measuring cup is in its own way repulsive and the antithesis of bonhomie and again slanderous to the bourbon. When my father and I opened a bottle of bourbon on Christmas Eve, it being for a while a tradition, my father made great drama of throwing the cap away. A gesture to the bourbon and the reality of two men taking a serious drink together.

'The measuring cup is cousin to the resealer. There are two types of barmen, too, in relation to the measuring cup. One who pours very carefully and to the precise volume of the cup, and the other who holds the cup over the glass and allows overflow. Civilised drinkers are "overflow" people.

'These items have no business on your trolley.'

THE SOULS
OF ANIMALS

To: Voltz@aol.com
Subject: the souls of animals

I was watching ABC (US) news and saw an item about how many
Americans believe dogs have souls (47%) and there was a shot
of an animal cemetery in the US where one of the buried dogs
was named Martini. I felt this was not proper. Don't know how
you feel about this. I like dogs, but Martini is not a dog's name.

From: Voltz@aol.com
Subject: the souls of animals

Agreed. Martini is not an appropriate name for a dog.

THE THIRTEEN AWARENESSES

Let us now consider the ritual of the martini, which in some ways parallels the Japanese tea-drinking ceremony but I will not stretch this analogy.

There are thirty-seven ways of touching the *lingam* and eighty to a thousand for the *yoni*, and I consider that there are probably thirteen awarenesses in the drinking of the martini. Some connoisseurs break it down into twenty-three distinct moments but I feel that this is going too far.

The *entry* into the right bar with the right people at the right time of the day is probably the equivalent to what is known in the tea-ceremony as *chumon* or the middle gate. Passing through the middle gate leaves behind, at least for a time, the frantic material world and we enter the calm space of contemplation and fellowship. Passing through the middle gate should bring about a changed demeanour from that of the work world. And the demeanour which overtakes us on any given day having passed through the middle gate, determines many things: whether we sit at a stool or a banquette, for example, whether we seek company or find being *among* people is all we required at that point of mood.

The next awareness comes at the *deliberations*. The martini is the only drink where it is acceptable, perhaps even a requirement, for there to be a discussion with the bartender about the crafting of the drink and where it is also acceptable, perhaps a requirement, that the drinker watch and appraise and respect the making of the first martini of the evening. Voltz has argued that in the past, that we should let the alchemists do their work in secret. It is true that some people choose not to know what goes into their cocktail, especially the post-modern cocktails. With a great bartender, the *deliberations* can go in many existential directions other than the making of the drink itself.

The next awareness is the *advent* of the drink as it is delivered to our place at the bar or at a table following the *deliberations*, the moment when the drink leaves the bartender and is transferred to us and, in all its elegance, it exists then for us and for us alone.

Part of this awareness is the careful delivery by the bartender of a brimful glass, without spillage, without theatre, but with ceremony.

Ideally, for the *advent*, the coaster will be neutral. A garish advertising coaster can spoil this moment. I do not agree with Voltz that it is safer to carry one's own plain or favourite coaster to a bar.

A plain paper napkin, which Voltz and other Americans call a 'bev nap' – beverage napkin – delivered with the drink is one of the good innovations of the American drinking culture. It is for the wiping of the mouth, the blotting of lipstick, for wiping condensation from the base of the glass, for use in case of spillage, and, for some, a place to enfold the olive pip out of sight.

As you know, I do not usually mix with people who indulge in match or bev-nap games. For anthropological reasons I will give an example of a bev-nap game – The Drunken Crab. Take a paper napkin and open it up. Twist all four points into legs. This is your crab. Now borrow a lemon or lime from the bartender and place it under the napkin and sculpt the napkin into the carapace of the crab. You could draw eyes and other features on it if you wish. Now gently roll the lime or lemon and watch the crab crawl across the bar.

If there are more futile ways of handling loneliness, boredom or emptiness, I don't know of them.

The *advent* is closely related to the *contemplation*. Some would argue that it is the same phase as the *contemplation*. This is, the moment where we turn our gaze exclusively to the martini and appreciate it as a visual image, an archetype, a tableau, an old friend. We see the martini there on the bar or at our table as near to perfect as possible at that moment in time and circumstance and history.

The art historian Kenneth Clark says we can enjoy a purely aesthetic sensation for only as long as we can keenly savour the smell of a fresh-cut orange – he estimates two seconds. Do not extend the *contemplation* much past that.

Closely following the *advent* and the *contemplation* comes a train of feelings which in turn trigger the moment of *affiliation*.

This is the affiliation with the martini and its long tradition referred to earlier when discussing Paglia's idea of gesturalism. The sensation of *affiliation* is not always the same sensation, and perhaps never the same. For example, sometimes when I drink a martini alone I feel I am in an Edward Hopper painting, say *Nighthawks* in which people are sitting at a bar or a diner, late at night.

When I mentioned this to Voltz once in the bar of the Four Seasons, he argued that 'people don't drink in Hopper paintings. They're always in hotel lobbies or in their rooms – but never in bars. Hopper really isn't the painter of the introspective drinker. You'd have to look for some French painting in the cubist style, say Leger or Braque or one of those guys.'

'Look, Voltz,' I said, 'I apologise if I am misusing Hopper. I am talking about a mood I get when I conjure up a Hopper painting while having a drink or when it conjures me up. And by the way, I don't see the banal negative curatorial conceptions of, say, "loneliness" in Hopper paintings, say, *Hotel Room* which shows a woman sitting on a bed in a chemise reading what may be the room service menu, perhaps about to order up a drink. I see solitariness. Not loneliness.'

There's nothing wrong with solitariness unless you don't want it. Yes, Voltz, I do realise that the setting of *Nighthawks* is probably a diner and not a place where you would normally expect to be served a martini. Did you know that Hopper went to Paris in 1906 when everything happening in art was happening there. When asked about this visit, Hopper said, 'Whom did I meet? Nobody. I'd heard of Gertrude Stein, but I don't remember having heard of Picasso at all. I used to go to the cafés at night and sit and watch.'

The next is the *elevation* of the drink, an awareness of our command of the drink. This is done with three fingers and thumb on the stem; generally, the little finger should be kept in close to the other three without touching the stem, although holding of the little finger out from the drink does give a nice effeminacy or old-style femininity to the hold if you are so inclined.

'Hand ostentatiously balancing garland and hem, a woman passed . . .' as Charles Baudelaire once wrote.

The taking of the drink into your hand and holding it and then the *elevation* of it, is both a claiming of it and a commitment to it. By taking it in hand we know that shortly we will be moved into a different sphere of self – it is a signing-on to the quest of all that the martini suggests, sponsors and lures.

Connoisseur Huon Hooke says the weight and grip of the glass, especially through the stem, should give you the sense of 'control' of the glass and, perhaps, of the future relationship between yourself and the drink, a doubtful view of this most unpredictable of partnerships. A good stem also gives you control of the swirling, in the case of wine, before taking in the bouquet, and in the case of the martini, for contemplative swirling or even for frivolous twirling as well. Because of the cone shape of the martini glass it is unnecessary to put a finger under the glass to stop it slipping through your fingers.

The next awareness is the taking in of the *bouquet*. The martini, as with wine, pleases the four senses – sight, smell, taste, and in the clinking of the glasses or the shaking of the ice in the mixer, hearing. You may moisten your finger and make the glass ring but this is only excusable when you are past the fourth martini; you will probably by then also have made the Drunken Crab and laughed a lot to yourself.

Talking of *bouquet*, I am fond of the stories of American writer J.F. Powers who writes about priests. In a short story entitled 'Prince of Darkness' a priest is in the confession booth taking the confessions of a woman. Through the grille the priest smells the apple blossoms pinned to the woman's dress but he then catches another smell: 'At the heart of the apple blossoms another scent bloomed: gin and vermouth.' A priest with a well-practised nose for the martini.

The next awareness is *first savouring*, the sharp, cold piquancy of the first taste. This may persist for a number of sips – the martini is always sipped, never gulped or taken in mouthfuls, except on the rare occasions one might need to 'pig out'. There are thirty-five sips in a martini, though Voltz argues that with a return to the smaller glass which exists in his wonderland of some nostalgic past, there would be twenty-two sips. In this awareness of *first savouring*, the martini is felt on the lips, tongue, the face and then the spirit, in what I call the kiss of the drink. If the chill and the strength and the compounding of the martini are well harmonised, there is sometimes even a small *bite* with the kiss of the drink, which is felt around the nerves of the face. This is a reminder of the seriousness of the martini.

Physiologically, what takes place is a keening of the trigeminal nerve of the face and mouth. The trigeminal nerve carries sensory information from the mucous membranes of the mouth, cheek, the tongue, lower teeth. The trigeminal registers the sensory impact on the nerves of our mouth as distinct from flavour. The trigeminal nerve is the 'touch' of the mouth. It experiences coldness, heat, chilli, English mustard, mint, carbonation. In some gin and vermouth combinations there may be also a peppery sensation.

The impact of the first sips of a fine martini might be compared to what is known colloquially as 'brain freeze' or 'ice-cream headache', when your head starts to stab for a few seconds after taking in something very cold. But with the martini it is not only the coldness.

The *second savouring* is of flavour. Flavour is affected by the condition of the mouth and by mood. Anxiety changes flavour. Flavour comes from the interaction of five basic tastes: salty, sour, sweet, bitter and *umami* (identified by Professor Kikunae Ikeda in 1907) which is the flavour of protein, sometimes referred to as 'meaty' and which is particularly enhanced by monosodium glutamate to which it may be related. As we have discussed, the flavours of the martini are entirely botanical.

The *third savouring* comes later in the drink when it has softened and lost its sharp coldness, and as our tastebuds become relaxed or slightly anaesthetised, and the taste of the vermouth is now more apparent.

The *fourth savouring* is of the last sips from the drink when it has faded and warmed a little and often has a predominating olive or briny taste. The last sips belong to the olive.

The eating of the olive will play its part somewhere in the drinking. As previously discussed it is a private matter of preference although the nature of the olive and one's choice of olive protocol may be included in the *exegesis*. The *exegesis* (Dr Anderson's word) is the interpretation, with others or with self, of the qualities of the drink in hand. But a warning: there quickly comes a time when the alcohol, the drink, should not be at the forefront of consciousness or conversation. Sometimes, for example, wine at a meal can be talked about for too long. The martini commentary likewise should never continue beyond the first five sips of the martini.

Finally, after going through the softening and the fading of the drink, you should at the conclusion of the first martini be able to hear the movement of the blood through the ears accompanied by a calmness, a stillness which begins to settle on the spirit together with *être bien dans sa peau* – a feeling of being at home in one's skin, as Xavier would say.

Also after the conclusion of the first martini it is not uncommon to experience what the Japanese call *aware* (not the English word) which is a feeling of poignancy at the inevitable passage of time towards death. Or anyhow, some sort of poignancy. Any sort of poignancy is good. Leave a fraction of space for *aware* in the drinking of the first martini.

If you are in the mood you may want to leave space also to glance at the other imps which swim in every martini – to feel the delicious bewilderment of being alive on a planet surrounded by unimaginable infinite space and unimaginable time; to experience once again the angst of living with an imperfect intelligence, and incomplete knowledge, and a consciousness prone to all weathers of the soul, and which is unable to answer the fundamental adolescent questions of our children about why we are here, why we exist; to laugh at the dangerous, nonsensical, religious narratives we concoct to handle all this; and the nature of inescapable death.

Or you may not, as the case may be.

> And time, that takes survey of all the world,
> Must have a stop.   *Henry IV*

The second martini does not require the same ceremonial observance as the first. It is a more expansive drink and leads to a wider conversational state, or if alone, down existential passageways, through the closed doors to a secret inner library of the mind.

You may go through momentary states of repentance and redemption. I'd trust them. You may find yourself saying, 'My guilt is inexpressible and the situation without remedy.' If you find yourself saying this aloud to yourself, it is advisable to take another drink and find yourself a companion or fellowship.

And you may find that you give a thought to our times of being unloved: 'The perpetual hunger to be beautiful and that thirst to be loved which is the real curse', as Jean Rhys wrote. As Jean Rhys discovered, life can be quite good without a single all-consuming love. And anyhow, true love is the answer for about half the population for half the time. Many husbands and wives feel unloved. But I wouldn't use Jean Rhys or myself as life models.

What is a clubbable condition of mind? Conversation should attempt wit (failed wit is fine); there should be a curious anecdote; some carefully carried new information from the work of the day; a newly reasoned position on the affairs of the world, or a surprising relinquishment of a long-held position; or the sharing of angst in a novel or humorous way. The mischievous act of gossip-telling, as well as its content, always confirms to me the exhilarating frailties of the human condition.

I have found there are those whose company brings out the truth and those who deter the truth, as there are those whose company magically increases our vocabulary and unlocks our knowledge and our wit. When the stimulation of good company is combined with alcohol, the alcohol itself behaves differently. Other things must be released by the body – adrenalin, serotonin – for alcohol to be at its best. Mirth is always welcome.

I become sad about the imperfections of life most when I hear myself failing my own sought-for human exchanges at the cocktail hour, especially when my conversation becomes intellectually unsafe, reckless in an uncreative way. The martini, however, helps correct failings or obliterates them.

I suppose there is the daily question of whether to drink or not to drink. With whom to drink. To what end? To advance a project or to just play the fool or both. We didn't plan our days when younger. The day 'unfolded'. I don't think I had a forward planner or diary. Things just happened without foresight. We were less discriminating about our company, I seem to recall, and drinking was a way of washing the blood off our togas.

A TYPICAL MARTINI EXCHANGE

Nearly every time I mentioned this book to someone, they would give me a joke or a story.

The Honourable Gordon Samuels told me this one.

A nun comes into a bar, pulls up a bar stool, and says to the bartender, 'I'd like a martinus straight up.'

He says, 'Sister, don't you mean a "martini"?'

The nun says, 'If I wanted more than one, I would've asked for it.'

Gordon's wife, Jackie Kott, an actress, then came into the conversation and said she remembered as a young wife making martinis for one of her first dinner parties. The first two martinis took away her hostess nerves and she had a third, and then heard herself say to those she'd been chatting to, 'I could do with some food — when on earth are they going to serve dinner?'

THE MYSTERIES

We arrive now at the mysteries of the martini.

During the time of my youthful marriage and my confused husbandhood, which I have mentioned and about which I may have told too much, I was working as a reporter on a newspaper in a country town. I had a second mentor in the town (not a lover), that is, other than Paul, a man named Penfold (it seems in recollection that he was always referred to as 'Penfold'). He had one of the most analytically penetrating minds I'd encountered up to my then twenty years of age.

The University of Sydney in those days sometimes based a lecturer in the larger country towns to teach in adult education classes which were organised by local committees of the Workers' Educational Association. In this town, it was Penfold, and we held him in high regard. He had degrees in law and arts and was a heavy drinker. He had broad interests but saw himself as a scholar of politics and international affairs.

I was to follow Penfold into adult education where I became an administrator and a tutor with the WEA and a few years later, after I'd left the town, Dr Anderson was to take over Penfold's adult education duties there.

I became Penfold's drinking companion and he in turn became my personal tutor for two years while I studied as an external student at the University of Queensland. His best adult education work was sometimes to enter the bar at around midday or earlier with all the newspapers, copies of *Foreign Affairs*, *The Economist*, *The Atlantic Monthly*, *Nation*, and whatever other magazines had come into his life over the last few days. He would sit at the bar, order his middy of beer and then begin to read the newspapers and journals. After his first beer he would then engage the nearest drinkers in conversation about the day's news. Or more than likely they would engage him. Within an hour there would be a few drovers, a few shearers, a few council workers, a few retired schoolteachers, bums and layabouts and whoever else might turn up, engaged in a discussion with Penfold who would sometimes refer to his journals, reading from them, explaining terminology and introducing concepts. He had been a member of the Communist Party but had abandoned it and become anti-communist.

One afternoon Penfold blundered drunk into the house where Paul and I lived and discovered Paul and me in bed having sex and then blundered out. The three of us never discussed it.

One of the propositions that I remember Penfold arguing was that it didn't matter which subject he taught, he would always be teaching the same subject, what he called the method of inquiry, even, he'd say, if he taught flower arrangement or, I suppose, the nature of the martini.

He argued that regardless of where you begin, any subject, if approached the right way, would carry you into all the great questions of life. Take flower arrangement. What is beauty? Botany and the structure of nature. Why this flower and not another? The economics of horticulture. Aesthetics and theories of interior design. Folklore and the role of flowers as political symbols and in coats of arms. The War of the Roses. The great questions of civics and politics. Why do we bother to 'arrange' flowers? How should we live? He also believed that in adult education there were no silly questions. Any question contained a pathway to something interesting and relevant.

So while drinking a martini I sometimes stare into it and remember Penfold. What is it, I say to him, that we can learn from the martini? I suppose we can just get drunk, or meander off in less awesome directions and see only the 'dancing myriads of winking eyes'. We don't *have* to learn from the martini.

But if we were so inclined I can hear Penfold say, well, the first is The Lesson of Elegant Simplicity: how fine the simplicity of the martini can be in an otherwise congested and over-elaborated existence full of things, full of the need for ownership of things, conspicuous consumption and the demands of life performance, of life competence. Should we spend more time at the gym and when there, are we doing it right? Should we somehow put more into our friendships? Should we spend, or have spent, more time with our children? Have we got our values right? Is our life 'in balance'? Should we

know more about tantric sex? Would it brighten up our lives?
Should we meditate? Should we diet harder? Should we give
more to those in hardship?

In this congested existence, the martini – in its classic glass,
icy cold and frosty, with its toothpick and olive, aesthetically
elegant, containing the fire of life within its iciness – stands out
as a way of denying these demands of life and the complications
of possessions. It is a way of focusing on something that will
bring us to calm and stillness. The American satirist from the
1930s H.L. Mencken said that the martini is 'the only American
invention as perfect as a sonnet' (and there we have Mencken
claiming the martini as an American invention).

However, as we observe this seeming perfection we know at
the back of our minds – and this, Penfold would say, is the
burden of knowledge – that in such an elegant and seemingly
simple creation as the martini there is The Lesson of Infinite
Nuance.

As I have drunk the martini over the years I never cease to be
dazed by the possibilities of variation within the simple classic
martini.

Voltz told me this story. 'I had dinner with a woman friend
from Vancouver who said that the most popular bar there, West,
has a bartender who will mix you a martini based on his reading
of your character – he calls it a "signature martini". So he looked
at her and what she was wearing, asked her some questions,
and then mixed it up – she said he referred to her qualities of
reticence, and so on, as he was mixing the martini. He made her
a vodka and mango concoction. I asked her if he put vermouth
in it and she said, "No, it was really just a vodka infusion."'

I found it interesting that this guy in Vancouver was advertising himself as a specialty martini-maker and mind-reader.

'A martini isn't a "specialty" drink; it's a drink with a certain purity: you should always know what you're getting, although occasionally one will be especially well-made and will stand out,' Voltz grumbled.

'Ah,' I said, 'but there's the mystery of it. Sometimes for reasons we cannot detect one martini will stand out.'

There is a release that comes from recognising the mysteries of variation in the martini. It is this: regardless of the variations that are open to us, we can carefully and in a precise way mix the defined versions of a classic martini and every time it will come out tasting different.

Thus this infinite nuancing inherent in the martini means that *no two martinis can ever be strictly the same.* Too many variations are always in play: the twenty or so botanicals; the different olives, let alone the salt and that lactic acid that might make their merry way into the martini from the olive brine; the temperature of the drink; even of the regional variations in the water from which the ice was made; the proportions of gin and vermouth; even the atmosphere of the bar in which it is drunk; the city (or train) in which it is drunk; the company in which it is drunk. Perhaps even the season – Lake Tahoe in the Fall.

Dr Anderson, for example, even more than Voltz, ponders the weather, and wonders in which weather is it not wise or happy to drink a martini, although he admits that he knows of no weather in which it is wrong to drink a martini, nor season.

In the blending of these twenty or so flavours we lose the multiplicity of flavours but in return we receive a unique, single flavour. Once blended, the flavours cannot be chased and rediscovered by taste. Do not try to find the botanicals. Just let your palate register the particular, singular martini in your hand, at the time.

A martini may remind you of another martini. I was having a martini with Dr Anderson on a hot February day at the Bayswater Brasserie when he said that the drink and the weather reminded him of a martini he had on an island of Hawaii about five years before. He could not remember the name of the island but he sure as hell remembered the martini.

The paradox, then, is that while the drink appears so simple and while its perfection seems so attainable, it is far from simple, and far from perfectly achievable. In fact, in its nuancing it teaches The Lesson of Tantalising Elusiveness.

Every time it is served, the martini represents a journey towards an unattainably ideal drink.

However, I rush to say, that does not take away from the fact that we drink remarkably fine martinis at times, even if they are just, just, always an infinitesimal distance from perfection – paradoxically and thankfully, it can be also an *imperceptible* distance from perfection.

Take the question of coldness. This ideal state for the martini – as cold as domestic refrigeration can make it, or the nearest we can get to it – exists just after it is made, exists perhaps for minutes at the most at the *advent*, but from then on it is warming up. But this warming of the martini by our hand should be seen as part of its nature. From the time we begin to drink the martini, the chill is going from the drink; the illusion of its pristine perfection is fading before us as we reach out to grasp it.

The martini, then, is always in a transitory state – what is known as The Sadness of Evanescence: to fade from sight; to become effaced, from the Latin *evanescere, vanus* meaning to become empty. It is astounding that the human mind is able to conceive of this perfection, to *imagine* the perfect martini, and then to accept that it is unattainable, and then to acknowledge that the imperfection can at times be imperceptible, and yet still continue to seek it without falling into madness. Maybe we do fall into madness. I suspect that Voltz is mad.

Oscar Wilde said that since *Hamlet* the world has been sad in a new way. Maybe since the martini the world has been calmed, intrigued and, at the same time, made happily world-weary in a different way. Maybe the martini represents the modernist consciousness and now, at the same time, through its contrast to The Crazy Drinks and their challenge, is also enfolded into a post-modern consciousness.

Anyhow, this, I hope, is the message we send to our children every time we drink a martini. And if it isn't, it means that the terrorists have won.

And so we reach the ultimate paradox: there is no such thing as *the* martini.

Yet there is a story that dedicated martini drinkers love to tell, which has been told to me over and over again in many bars, and was first told to me by David Catterns – Harry's father – many years ago, after his first visit to New York. Martini Drinker comes into bar, orders a martini. Bartender says, vodka or gin? The Martini Drinker says, just a martini. Bartender says, olive or twist? Martini Drinker says, just a martini. 'Straight up or on the rocks?' Martini Drinker says, just a martini. Bartender goes away and comes back with a gin martini, some vermouth, straight up with a single olive on a toothpick. The bartender *knew* but didn't know he knew.

The story is a folktale that works on the illusion that there is only *one* martini.

There is a more pointed version. In the film *Deep Impact*, the actress Téa Leoni has had a bad day and goes to a bar and orders, 'A martini. Up. Big.'

As we have seen, historically too, it has never been the same thing – Jack London, Ian Fleming, Dorothy Parker and Kurt Vonnegut were drinking different martinis.

The martini exists only as versions of itself, both defined versions, and random versions caused by random factors.

It is The Lesson of the Paradox of Jacky's Axe, which Dr Anderson says is taken from a now deceased cartoonist named Eric Jolliffe and his cartoon series entitled 'Saltbush Bill'. In one of the cartoons, Jacky is chopping wood and the boss comes by and says, 'That's a fine axe you got there, Jacky.'

'Yes, boss,' says Jacky, 'this is the best axe I ever used. Only three new handles and one new head in all the time I had it.'

The 'axe' has continuity as an idea, a perfect abstract type, not as an object. So does the martini.

As the Greek philosopher Heraclitus said, the road up and the road down are one and the same but are not seen as such. Yeah, right, Heraclitus, thanks, and yet everything flows and nothing stays. But we go on with our lives, nevertheless.

Maybe it's something else other than the *drink* that we are trying to capture when we drink the martini. Not only are we in search of a perfect martini, we are in search of a transmuting potion that will take us to another state of existence. Now, in the at times unliveable 21st Century, we are, perhaps, hoping it will take us to another time and another world – say a bar car on a train in 1940 with the landscape receding. As well, of course, taking us to solace, transcendence, temptation and folly.

And we can meet the uncontrollable variations with a curious openness.

I have mentioned the pleasing world-weariness of the martini, the resigned state of being jaded. The martini is relaxed about the struggle along the path of enlightenment: it parodies the path of enlightenment. It has become part of the custom of the martini drinker to dissect every aspect of the drink, so much so that discussion about the martini often becomes cabbalistic. I wrote earlier that you may eat the olives in a martini any old way, even unthinkingly, but I said that this does go against the martini game. Nothing about the martini is to be done 'unthinkingly'.

The martini is both a simple demonstration and a parody of the Platonic dictum that the unexamined life is not worth living.

But these esoteric discussions and stories and martini folklore are a pathway. They are a pathway into conversation with an old friend, or with a stranger in a bar. The martini sponsors fellowship, and fellowship and storytelling are our only solace from existential terror.

I once asked Voltz whether the martini could ever be drunk ironically. He replied that the martini was quarantined from irony because there had to be one part of our lives that was exempt from irony. He'd chosen the martini.

'Sure, there are martini jokes,' he said, 'but why waste time talking about it *ironically*? The rest of the world can be talked about ironically. That's enough. And another thing, if you tried to talk about the martini ironically, it would enfold the irony.'

❦

I have given talks about the martini — at the Sydney Writers' Festival, two at M-on-the-Bund in Shanghai, two at the Hong Kong International Literary Festival.

I have been to quite a few literary festivals around the world but I have never been to one where three of the four Horsemen of the Apocalypse were also present: war, pestilence, and death — they were there at the Hong Kong Festival. On the day the festival began, news hit of a 'killer flu', called at first atypical pneumonia and later SARS, which had hit hundreds of people in Hong Kong and about which WHO had just issued a world-wide alert.

Having just checked in when I heard this, I headed for the Sonata bar, a highrise hotel bar in Hong Kong overlooking the bay and the glittering teeming life of the city. With some sense of calamity — it was the first time I had been caught in a plague — I took with me the newspapers full of news of this mystery illness sweeping the island and perhaps the world.

I ordered myself a martini, discussed the making of it with the barman, and went to a table.

Nearby, I saw a man, sitting, head in his hands, with a martini in front of him. I guessed that he might be also a guest at the festival and, because of the martini, I asked him. He was.

We joined up and as I sat down he said, 'I see you have stuffed olives in the martini. Don't you find that the capsicum is a little too, how should I say, colourful? That red spot in the glass?'

Oh God, I thought, it's Voltz's brother. And then I thought, it's the red blood spot of the plague. I told him and we laughed. His name was Jon Cannon and he rang through to his wife, the novelist Lui Hong – *Startling Moon* – and she came up to the bar with their three-year-old Ann and also ordered a martini.

Together we sat there looking out over Hong Kong Bay, over the whole world, drinking our martinis, and joking with bravado about the plague sweeping the island, recalling Thomas Mann's *Death in Venice* in which the authorities try to keep the news of the plague a secret so as not to spoil the tourist season: 'There is no plague in Venice'.

Lui and Jon had to make a decision whether to stay or go and decided that the flight out on the aircraft might present more of a risk than staying in Hong Kong.

Given my private low state of mind, it didn't seem to matter whether I stayed with the plague or left. My old mate, the remarkable Richard Hall, historian, former private secretary to Prime Minister Gough Whitlam, was dying in Royal Prince Alfred Hospital and I was back in therapy.

The next day there were people in the streets wearing masks.

The news then was that hundreds were infected and dying.

Ten writers had cancelled.

I was on the program to give my lecture entitled 'The Martini Dialogues'. On the night of my first appearance, the American invasion of Iraq began, and people at the festival started talking of a new world war — 'the clash of civilisations'.

I acknowledged to the audience that it could be seen as extraordinarily decadent to be talking about the right way to make a martini in the midst of a plague surrounded by who knew how many dead and dying and at the outset of a war of unknown magnitude and implication. And myself in therapy again. And Richard Hall dying.

I did know, however, that the bon vivant Richard Hall, although not himself a martini drinker, would approve of me giving the talk.

The internationally famous Dr Meghan Morris, a professor in cultural studies at Lingnan University, rose from the audience and said that she considered my willingness to talk about the martini and the presence of a full house to hear it in the famous M on the Fringe restaurant was, 'an affirmation of the good life in the face of the human condition'. The audience and I applauded her.

And the audience was jolly, despite the collapsing world outside. When I was in China in the 1980s as a cultural ambassador, the themes of the visit were Brotherhood and Peace and International Friendship, which my Chinese hosts toasted in many speeches with many glasses of rice wine. As remarkable as Chinese cuisine is, it is limited in its combination of alcohol with food — there are no wines, no martinis. (I once said this to a Chinese communist apparatchik and it sent her into a rage.) But, now, at least, I was able to help correct that. Here I was, back in China, teaching them how to mix a martini. Maybe I was a tipping point in the history of China and would topple them into decadence.

Together that night, the audience, three Horsemen of the Apocalypse and I pondered the mysteries of the martini.

A week later, after the last performance of my martini lecture in Shanghai, the Consul-General Sam Gerovich took me aside and said they had received news that day that Richard Hall had died but had kept it from me until after my lecture.

I thanked him and then took my martini out on the balcony of the restaurant looking down on the Yangtze River and the moving lights of its interminable river traffic, and remembered Richard and all the drinking, dining and arguments we had shared since we were seventeen.

I recalled two things Richard taught me. When we were young cadet journalists we were talking about sex. He was a Catholic and I an atheistic socialist. I do not know what sexual experience he'd had and although I'd had very little it was, well, already *varied*. I remember him saying, 'Sex is a tangible expression of the intangible.' I liked that. I was to learn that it is sometimes the tangible expression of the tangible and that that's fine too.

Later in our lives after he'd gone into politics, we were talking about government funding of the arts. I was interested in how we could convince people and politicians that the arts were important and worth funding. We looked at arguments about art being the 'memory of the nation' and that avant-garde art taught people how to think creatively; that it was important for a culture to 'have its own stories'.

At the end of the discussion, he said, 'I'm afraid a belief in the value of the arts is a matter of faith,' and then he laughed. 'Tell that to Caucus. Tell that to the electorate.'

Richard did tell them. And they did believe him.

Richard did not drink spirits at any time in his life. He believed that by sticking to beer and wine he would not become an alcoholic. He died of medical complications aggravated and almost certainly caused by alcohol, but his mind was in great shape through to the end.

My last meeting with him was in hospital just before I left for Hong Kong and Shanghai. He wanted to piss. I said that I would get a nurse but he mumbled, 'You do it.' I found the urine bottle and pulled down the bedding, pulled down his pyjamas, and put his penis into the bottle. I said, 'After this I will get you a copy of *Playboy* and we can do the other thing.'

He laughed, in a sick, constricted way. 'Don't make me laugh, it hurts.'

Richard was a very traditional male. He and I had never shaken hands, put our arms around each other's shoulder, hugged, let alone cheek-kissed affectionately, even in that new male way we were supposed to adopt in the days of liberation back in the 1970s.

The holding of his penis and putting it in the urine bottle is, I think, the only physical contact I ever had with him during nearly fifty years of knowing him as a close friend.

I left the balcony, went back inside to the milling crowd and had another martini.

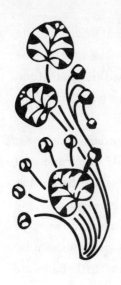

WHERE ARE THEY NOW?

And what has happened to those lively and, for me, hugely significant people who inspired the characters in the story that began this memoir, the chapter 'Martini' from my book *Forty-Seventeen*? And the others who came to mind during the writing, those people from my youthful days which this memoir bring to my mind again as I sit here with a martini.

My Male Lover. My lover from my teenage years, Paul J., who wanders through this memoir, is married with grown children, and, until recently, was still my lover. He says he has never had any other gay relationship. He hardly drinks now and anyhow never drank martinis. He does not read the *New Yorker* any more.

Trevor the Solicitor. I do not know what happened to Trevor the solicitor who took my anal virginity when I was a teenager after I had flirted with him and played hard-to-get. We did arrange to meet again some ten years later in the city when I was twenty-eight; before the drinks I'd had sexual fantasies about being with him again, but I found he was no longer interested in me. I was too old, or the passing of time had changed things. I wrote a story about the meeting entitled 'Ten Years', in *Futility and Other Animals*.

The Older Woman. The older woman, Norma Crinion, who taught me, among many things, how to make a martini, died from lung cancer at about sixty. A paradoxical woman, she was educated at Monte Sant'Angelo Mercy College, an exclusive Catholic Girls' School, but became a communist in the dying days of the Party in the 1980s after working as an executive secretary of the Institute of Directors. I remember that she once became fed up with a job she had and asked me to call them and tell them she'd been killed in a road accident and go and pick up some books from her desk.

Some nights she would telephone me and ask me to come around and if I couldn't come, she would ask me to 'be a darling' and call the cab, give money and tip to the cab driver, and ask him to buy her a cooked chicken, a two-litre flagon of wine, a carton of cigarettes, and deliver them to her. She never married. During her life, she was a lover of some of my friends, including Penfold and Dr Anderson, and of some people with high media profiles. She once went to a drive-in to see a must-see film with film theorist and actor John Flaus, then an impoverished student. Neither of them owned a car so they took a taxi (for which she paid) and were prepared to sit on the ground in a car space on a blanket, however the owner of the drive-in loaned them two chairs and they sat together on the chairs in a car space and watched the movie.

She was manager of the newspaper *City Voices*, which I started and edited.

She said around the time of her death that she wasn't worried about dying: 'I have always had an on-and-off relationship with life.'

Jenny the Poet. The poet Jennifer Rankin died in 1979 at thirty-eight of cancer. Before she died, when she was just becoming sick from the cancer, we did a reading tour together in Tasmania. On our arrival we were taken to the house of a poet where we were to stay. I looked around and pronounced the accommodation unacceptable for sick Jennifer (and for snobbish me). From then on we booked ourselves into the best hotels in whatever town we were staying and sent the bill to the sponsor of the reading tour.

While on the tour, we visited a church near where the painter John Glover had lived in the 1830s and which he had used, and we signed our names in the visitor's book. Jenny wanted us to play 'Bride and Bridegroom' and we went to the altar and stood there holding hands and she had us go through the marriage vows from the Book of Common Prayer she found in a stack at the back of the church. After we went through the words of the ceremony she took on the voice of a minister and said, 'You may kiss the bride' and we kissed. She said that staying in the hotels was our honeymoon, but we did not have sex on that tour.

As she approached death she told me that she was giving up chemotherapy and taking on natural cures and meditation. I said to her, 'Jenny, do both.' She said if she did, the natural cures wouldn't work. It would be bad faith.

During her development as a poet, she befriended Galway Kinnell and Ted Hughes, and it was Galway in a bar in Honolulu who told me that she had died. She married the painter David Rankin, who now lives in New York, and together they raised Thomas.

No one seems to know the whereabouts of Thomas, who was one and two when I knew him.

Penfold. Penfold ended up as a professor in the Department of Law at the University of New South Wales. He died of lung cancer in his fifties. We met only once after we'd both left the country. Recently a couple of his children came to see me asking me to tell them more about their father who had left the marriage when they were young.

The Young Girl. The young girl in the story 'Martini' evolved from my relationship with Fiona Giles. She was the girl whom I taught to make a martini when she was eighteen, married *her* high-school boyfriend, was unfaithful to him with me, divorced him at twenty-seven, joined up with the Older Man – me – and we went to live in Oxford while she did her doctorate.

After a few stormy and exhilarating years Fiona and I split up and my heart was broken and I went into therapy three days a week for three years (which, of course, was about my problems as shown up by the relationship, not about the relationship as such). She lived for a time in New York, and has edited two books of stories and has written two books and went on to marry and have two children. She hardly drinks and never really liked the martini.

Recently we found ourselves together on a panel at a writers' conference discussing the subject 'Intimate Journalism'.

As I sat and listened to her contribution and admired her, it crashed down on me that she and I should be talking about the book *Forty-Seventeen*. I had written it while living with her and in some ways it drew on our lives together but until that moment the book had not come into my consciousness although I had been fully aware that we would be together on the panel and having lunch together after the panel discussion.

After she had spoken and sat down, I passed her a note saying, 'Fiona, what about us in *Forty-Seventeen*?' She laughed.

It is the only one of my books that has no dedication because I did not want her life to be blighted by people saying, 'Oh, so you're the girl in *Forty-Seventeen*.'

Her personal copy is inscribed by me this way: 'This book is of course silently dedicated to you – only you and I know the true story.'

Recently we were having a drink together and talking about this book and she, in her forties, said, 'I now rather like the idea of being remembered as the young girl.'

My Young Wife. What of the young wife from the martini story and our life before we were arguing about martinis? Margaret and I had grown up in a country town, had known each other since about age five, went to the same Sunday school, went to the same infant, primary and high schools, the same church, and we married in that church to please our families, even though we were atheists. We read the *Communist Manifesto* together at high school.

She went on to two marriages and had two children by her second marriage and one by her third and has remained married for years now. She became a magazine editor in London. So much for 'I'm quite happy to be the country girl'. We are still in touch now and then.

Recently I was asked back to our former high school as a writer and I decided to read them a story based on our young love and about the school that they were attending and where the storytelling started. It was on this visit to the school that I had a stunning realisation that she too had A Story Not Told.

MEMOIR OF A STORY: STORY OF A MEMOIR

Noisy teenagers swirl by me in the corridor. They seem to flow around and passed me as a lifestream. I feel like a bear standing mid-river.

The 'old school' I'd known is obliterated by new buildings (back in my day it had just been built and was then the 'new' school). The new school is now my old school.

I was able to find Room 17 where I'd first kissed Margaret my girlfriend and put my hand on her breasts through her school uniform, the first breasts I'd touched since I was a baby. And we were to give each other our virginities (at least, I believe she was a virgin).

The teacher who had organised my visit to the school had not yet arrived and I found myself standing in front of the buzzing class. Some of the Year 11 girls had their nails varnished, some wore earrings in pierced ears and other jewellery. One girl even did the college toss with her shampooed and conditioned hair, as she looked at me standing uneasily in front of the class. I looked away.

When the teacher came in I felt that I was a student again, a student who'd been caught showing-off in front of the class. I felt I should sit down with the rest of the students and take out my books.

After the teacher had introduced me I told the students that I would read a chapter from one of my novels which told of my days at their school in the 1950s.

'In *Forty-Seventeen* a novel I wrote a few years ago, I have some letters written by a girl student at a high school to her boyfriend who left school the year before and has gone to the city to work on a newspaper.

'You don't have to be a mind-reader to know the boy in the story is based on me.

'The letters are a blending of imagination and factual record – I drew on the letters written to me by my then girlfriend and which I had kept. I thought they'd give you a taste of what it was like here at the high school back then – and maybe you can tell me what's changed.'

Could they even envisage me having a 'girlfriend'? Oddly, I felt sucked back through time to where I felt increasingly closer to their age. I felt somehow back at school. The sense of my contemporary self, or at least, my persona there today in front of the students – 'the writer' – was becoming unstable.

'I was a year ahead of her and I'd gone to the city to be a cadet journalist and she was finishing her final year of high school. She wrote to me every week throughout the school year. The letters provide a great picture of life at school back then. Maybe it will connect with the way you experience school now. Or maybe things have changed too much. We'll see. The story is entitled "A Portrait of a Virgin Girl".'

I looked up over my glasses. No tittering, no giggles.

'She is sixteen and I – I was seventeen.' Small sensations of being seventeen came to me, further loosening my shell of identity, dissolving any sense of my age. She was a virgin. And I? Not really, although there are quite a few virginities. I was a heterosexual virgin.

'Each letter in the story begins by repeating the first line as a refrain. I will begin now with her first letter to me.

'"*It's hard for me to say 'dearest'* . . . It's hard for me to say 'dearest'. I've never written real words of love before . . ."'

'Dearest'. Did that sound old-fashioned to them? 'Uncool'?

'"*Dearest, now there I've used the word* . . . Dearest, now there I've the used the word and I hope it makes you happier . . . Your letters are on the lounge room table when I get home from school and I then journey into my bedroom where I emotionalise . . ."'

Had it made her happy to use the word 'dearest'? I guessed not.

'"*At the local show I had a passion.* At the local show I had a passion after I watched a sideshow where there was a hypnotist . . . the idea of having a spell or a trance put on me is frightening as another part of me would like it very much methinks . . ."'

As I read, I remembered our heavy petting, and the trance of that, the feverish urge to surrender to our wilful bodies but the resistance offered by her judgement and by the fear rising from our sexual inexperience.

What lay ahead of us was our first sex, then the wilful wedding against our parents' advice, soon after we'd left school, the prickly confused marriage, the counselling, the long separation and then a flirtation with the idea of getting back together, the divorce, our curiosity about each other at our occasional, sometimes erotic reunions in London over the years, the unfolding of my true sexuality.

'"*Forgive me for being such a fool when you were home.* Forgive me for being such a fool when you were home. I said some stupid things and I hurt you . . . you know the whole time what it was I was scared of – that one thing leads to another from saying 'I love you' and I wasn't ready for the physical thing which comes from saying it . . ."'

I broke into the story to tell them that Margaret and I had 'indulged in heavy petting' down in the long grass at the edge of the playing fields while on prefect duty. 'I see that the long grass has now been cut.'

I laughed. They didn't. No expressions on the faces of Year 11.

'"*It was really great to be a 'real girlfriend'.* It was really great to be a 'real girlfriend' with you in the city last weekend. As much as I wanted to amaze them I didn't tell Mum and Dad about going with you to the Greek Club and having the glass of wine . . ."

'"*I was in the Dainty-Lingerie shop this morning* . . . I was in the Dainty-Lingerie shop this morning returning something (never mind what) and inside there was a woman buying a nightdress and her husband was there giving approval on her selection. It was funny to see a man doing such a thing . . . I can't describe what it was that made me feel funny . . ."

'"*I'm sorry I forgot to read your short stories . . .* I'm sorry I forgot to read your short stories you sent me . . ."'

Even now a shot of pain passes through my heart. How could she have done that? To have received my first short stories and then not responded. Was she frightened of what she might read? Or was she bored with it all? Was it all too much for her? Why hadn't I got the message back then that all this was only some sort of trying-out of life for her, as it must have been for me, although we could never allow ourselves to think of it that way. And that she was now trapped in it. And what had I felt? I'd been driven by confused and hungry needs. Why had she gone along with it? Why had we ended up married? Why had I been driven to this girl, why had I persevered with such obsession? Was it because I loved her girlhood — was I trying to steal her girlhood?

'". . . And what is this 'mysterious story' you won't show me? When will I ever 'be ready' to read it . . .?"'

That was 'The Story Not Shown', written in that year, and which was to become another chapter in my novel *Forty-Seventeen* thirty years later and never shown or told to her. There were other 'Stories Not Told' from my first years in the city. This story describes my visit to a prostitute.

Retrospectively, I see that 'The Story Not Shown' was an immense psycho-diversion, an unconscious personality manoeuvre not comprehended by me as the young writer and beyond my self-analysis back then, a manoeuvre to make myself look away from myself as much as it was a way of not telling her about my self. It was an unconscious diversion from the silent, invisible and vicious in-fighting occurring in my personality. The story pushed something aside in my consciousness, smothered the other stories – the real stories untold.

The first of the stories untold was that the prostitute was an attractive, very feminine, youthful transvestite and that the sexual encounter was for me thrilling, arousing and presented to me a fantasy that I had never found within myself until then and that the appearance of this girl-boy and our youthful embrace seemed dazzlingly appealing and right. It was an awakening. At first I'd thought that the tranny was a female but soon I realised that this was not so and this itself had thrilled me. The young tranny was, in recall, pleased that I was close to her age and so attracted to her, yet she was also charmingly unpractised in the business she was in.

In 'The Story Not Shown', later published in the novel, the prostitute was changed to a woman from another time. From that untold fact flowed other pivotal stories untold to this day. 'The Story Not Shown' was a diversion from the other stories from my first year in the city which I could not tell to my school girlfriend nor tell to 'myself' – myself then being made up of the beginner-writer-self who at that time lacked the imaginative horse-whispering to corral the stories; and the heavy-drinking, nervous cadet journalist who was unable to tell the four stories to anyone and who locked those secret stories in a windowless barn of my mind. The self both unformed and deformed, unrecognisable and unrecognised, had *its* stories which, for then, were *inaccrochable.* But that self from that time should not be judged a lying self. Other more forgiving words need to be found.

When intimate couples pledge to always tell each other the truth about themselves – to be totally honest – they do not always realise how difficult it is to be descriptive and to be precise when you don't know what is true about yourself, let alone how to describe it or live with it. If I'd told Margaret the Stories Untold she would have almost certainly recoiled and bolted, and would have herself then been free – free of me. If I had had the self-comprehension and the personal agency and command to be able then to *tell* the stories, I would have also been freed perhaps, would have found the strength to open the barn, shepherding the other stories out into the world, into the dazzling light of my own self-comprehension. I would have gone on the stranger path not taken.

And it was a diversion from what had happened in my life with Paul. The other Story Not Told. At the time of the love letters referred to in the story, Paul had already come into my life. I had already seduced him in a hotel room in Kings Cross.

I paused in my reading of the story and looked at the students. I felt I should stop that reading and tell them these stories roaming in my head and how these stories were locked in a windowless room for so long. But I went on with the reading of my carefully disciplined 'story'.

'"*When I began to change to womanhood* . . . When I began to change to womanhood, Mum gave me some books and for the first time I've seriously looked at them and they convinced me that sexual relations between us now would ruin our life . . ."'

I couldn't look out at the students – how many of them had had sex? I wanted to say to them that it didn't have to 'ruin' your life. I then lifted my face to them and tried for a smile to say 'don't take that too seriously'.

'"... Mr W was talking to me after class and told me he once wrote a poem about love and, thinking that I would appreciate it, he let me read it after the others had gone ..."'

The sentence about the teacher and his love poem leapt up at me from the page. The teacher actually wanted her to stay back with him so that he could read her a very personal love poem? My God, had the teacher been coming on to her, making a tentative advance? Could that be true?

Back then – at the time I'd received the letter, this had not occurred to me. Nor had it occurred to me ten years ago while working from her letters as I wrote this chapter of the novel. It had never occurred to me that the teacher had begun to see her as a sexual being.

The teacher was probably only ten years older than she – although to us the teachers had seemed to be pretty much all of a single age, to belong to another chronology, out of reach.

Well, well. The teacher had been flirting with her. I had never read the letter that way.

I finished the story and asked Year 11 for questions. For comments. The students had none. I myself was filled with questions.

I looked out at them hoping they might cry out, 'It's just the same – you are one of us. Come and have a milkshake with us after school. Hang out with us.' I could start my life again.

But they were standing, picking up their bags.

At morning tea in the staff room, I said to the gathered teachers that the students didn't seem to respond to the story.

'Year 11 listen, but they don't always have much to say,' one of the teachers said.

'I wonder if any of it connected? They are probably much more cool these days.' Why was I saying 'cool'?

'Oh no, it sounded like their lives, all right.'

I then asked, 'What about the teacher wanting to talk with the girl after class and showing her his love poem? That would be frowned on these days?'

'Absolutely. We're all more nervous about that stuff.'

❧

Back in the city I told Matt about the meaning of the letter finally arriving, so to speak. 'There I was at the school and the letter finally arrived. This teacher – Mr W – was coming on to Margaret back then. Maybe W and Margaret had something going. Does it sound like that to you?'

'Sounds like it. When was all this?'

'When? At school. When she was at school. The year after my final year at high school.'

'But how long ago in years?'

I calculated. I had difficulty saying it. 'About forty years ago.'

'And the letter has just arrived?' Matt said. 'So to speak.'

'Yes.'

'Is it just left-over lover's paranoia, so to speak? Could it be that, do you think?'

'Could be that. Everything is so weird in my life these days that the commonplace has become unusual. But I like the idea that Mr W and Margaret had an affair. It gives symmetry to it all, gives a counterbalance to my sexual complications at the time. My Story Not Told.'

'If it's true, it's a good story.'

'It could *very well* be true: or it could have come very, very close to happening.'

'"Close to happening" is not to be easily dismissed. It is itself a narrative event.'

'Her Story Not Told. Maybe not even told to herself?'

It was intriguing and somehow pleasing in its narrative symmetry, that my young innocent girlfriend may have had a remarkable, secret Story Not Told from back then.

'Don't dwell on it,' Matt said, in closing.

I had lunch with two of my and Margaret's friends from the schooldays recently and they brought along photographs from that time. One was of Margaret in school uniform – starched white shirt, school tie, school tunic – aged sixteen. When I saw her my stomach turned over, both physiologically and poetically, at the photograph and at her beauty and youth and from the memory of our time together then, of the petting and swooning in private places and in the dark, as our childish bodies became sexually alive, and from the queer act of possession of her girlhood that I unconsciously attempted.

Which brings us now to Mr W.

Mr W. Mr W the school teacher who wanted to show Margaret his love poem, is now retired. That teacher, although he never taught me, was the most influential for her and for others in the school. He was a Christian Socialist and he introduced us, the school intelligentsia, to Fabian socialism. He also introduced me, through Margaret, to the poems of Carl Sandburg. When my father first visited New York he asked me if there was anything I wanted. I can remember no other time when he asked me to name my gift. I asked for the complete poems of Carl Sandburg, which he bought for me, even if a little perplexed that his young son wanted poetry (oh, oh).

'Why don't you just ask her whether anything happened?' Matt asked.

'I don't know. I think I'm frightened of her. Always was. She's so *grounded*. She thinks I'm screwy.'

'Frightened?'

'Disquieted. Sometimes, in some places, in some moods she still disquiets me.'

'We are quite right to be disquieted by the other sex, I suppose.'

'Panic-stricken. I'm frightened of some sorts of men. By the way, the teacher's still alive.'

'He is?'

'She writes to him.'

'They have an email relationship?'

'She writes letters to him.'

'He must be a hundred.'

'She writes to him. Yes. He's getting on. School students don't usually write to their teachers all their lives.'

'Ask them both. Have it out with them. Get the true story.'

'Ask my high school girlfriend whether she had an affair with a teacher when she was my girlfriend in high school? Or after?'

'That's my suggestion, yes. Get to the bottom of it. Find this thing called "closure" we hear so much about.'

'I want narrative symmetry more than this-thing-we-call-closure. I suppose I could ask Mr W as well. But he may put me on detention.'

In London last month Margaret and I dined at Mirabelle.

'I know Mirabelle isn't fashionable any more,' I said. 'We probably won't get our photographs in the paper.'

She looked at the menu. 'It's hugely expensive. Do you worry about getting your photograph in the paper?'

'I am still puzzled and surprised when it happens.'

She looked across at me. 'You mean that it happens?'

'It has happened. I have been photographed in restaurants and my photograph has appeared in the paper.'

'It's very expensive. We could have had something at my place.'

'We only get to eat together every twenty-five years.'

'I suppose that's true.'

The meal meandered on; how unbelievably out-of-reach she was to me.

I then said, 'Mr W had a crush on you. We all knew that.'

She blushed more deeply than any mature woman I had seen. 'I don't understand what you mean – a "crush"?'

'He was attracted to you. Attracted to you as a young woman coming alive – sexually.'

'But he was married. It was his first year as a teacher when he taught me. Through to the end of high school. He was the most important thing in my high schooling. Nothing *happened*, if that's what you mean. You'll have to explain to me about the "crush" he had on me – how do you know this?'

'Maybe you weren't tuned in to the signals then. Too young.'

'Nothing happened like in *Capturing the Friedmans*, if that's what you're alluding to. I think there were people casting "nasturtiums".'

I recalled but did not mention that she had excited the passion of another adult male back then who had to be sent packing by her parents when he turned up at her home.

Mr W once wrote to congratulate me when one of my books won a prize. He reminded me that he gave the speech at Margaret and my wedding. She invited him, obviously, as an act of adoration. He said that there was an error in the book – I mention 44-gallon petrol drums in 1936. He said that there were no 44-gallon drums before World War II.

Thank you, Mr W.

I realised after all this time that I had been hopelessly competing intellectually with him at high school. Worse, he was competing with me. He couldn't win a place in her social life: she was out of his respectable reach, too far out of her age group. But in private with her he would have won – what chance did I have of impressing my teenage girlfriend when I was competing against a charismatic Christian Socialist polymath and expert on 44-gallon drum history.

'Mr W made me a socialist,' she said, out of the blue, there in Mirabelle, 'and I still am.'

'No,' I said, '*I* made you a socialist. I read the *Communist Manifesto* to you after school in the lounge room of my home.'

'No, Mr W made me a socialist. He introduced me to G. D. H. Cole.'

'I made you a socialist one afternoon but I forgot to turn you back.'

'What is that supposed to mean?!'

'Oh, forget it. There are other more interesting positions than "being quote a socialist unquote".'

'I think it's an honourable position and one day the world will wake up to itself.'

I write to Mr W and ask him how 'special' Margaret had been in his life back then when we were all together at school. He wrote back something about her being 'a remarkable young woman'.

I tell Matt about Mirabelle and the letter from Mr W.

He says, well, that's that.

'What do you mean "that's that"? By not telling me, they might be protecting me. Protecting themselves?'

'You could let it go. Why don't you get back to your book?'

'Matt, this *is* the book.'

'I thought it was about the folklore of the martini.'

'The book is about what the book is about. I love the idea that there was something going on that I have never been told about. The narrative symmetry which we've discussed.'

'You know what?'

'What?'

'I don't think you're ever going to know if something happened. They're never going to tell you. That's the narrative symmetry. That's the justice of it. Or it could be that they did not know what was going on. Neither of them realised what it was or could admit it. Consider that for sym-metry. Symmetry of the undiscovered. Symmetry of the unknowable.'

'They were dabbling with taboo. I was also deep in taboo. I had one foot deep in taboo. I was wandering off further and further into taboo.'

'That's good – you are now wondering but wondering without pain, wondering with a unique piquancy. That's the symmetry. That's the piquant justice of it all.'

'Suppose that's a possibility. This fearful symmetry.'

'The fearful symmetry – you beat me to it.'

'Nature abhors perfection. I suppose it abhors symmetry as well.'

'I mean symmetry, "so to speak". And I don't think narrative abhors it.'

'She says it's all in my head.'

'I don't want to feed your paranoia, but she would say that, wouldn't she?'

Another feeling came creeping up from my buried past. I was not competing with him only for Margaret, I was also competing with *Margaret* for Mr W's affections. Although he didn't teach me, he was very alive in my consciousness at school and I carry a strong attractive image of him, blond hair brushed forward over his forehead in that private school way of those times.

More importantly, as my therapist might point out, the three of us, Margaret, he and I, are still strangely – directly and indirectly, consciously and unconsciously – interacting, all these forty years later, perhaps, still, with very little understanding of what was happening back then.

'Matt, remember that school teacher who competed with me for Margaret's affections at school – the story "Memoir of a Story: Story of a Memoir" – who challenged the accuracy of me mentioning 44-gallon drums before World War II?

'At last I've found a photograph taken in Christchurch, New Zealand, circa 1930, and the caption reads: "A Highways transport Leyland truck carrying a load of petrol in 44-gallon drums. Circa 1930".

'I have now sent this photograph to her to send on to Mr W.

'The photo also shows that there is always something to do in New Zealand. Always something to photograph. There is always something going on in New Zealand.'

Why do I feel the need to have a cheap shot at New Zealand?

While I was at the Hong Kong Literary Festival giving my martini lecture, Margaret sent me an email from London with the subject title: 'Hong Kong and martinis', which read, 'I can't quite gather from your email whether you are still in the hellhole of SARS and when your speaking engagements – about martinis??? – will take place. We were planning to go to Hong Kong but have cancelled.'

What hellhole? I was in the Sonata bar most of the time drinking martinis with Jon Cannon and Lui Hong.

Her email went on, 'You say that your state of mind is low, I find it strange that you should be lecturing around the world about the martini. I don't remember that you ever drank martinis when we were together. Is this lecturing on the martini what you do now?'

Margaret often excites in me a perverse desire to tell her that her worst predictions about me have come true. So in my reply, I confirmed that lecturing about the martini cocktail, literature and film in dim bars and nightclubs around the world, was pretty much what I did now – it was not the way I'd intended to use my life. I told her that Rob O'Neill had recently been quoted in a newspaper talking about how things turned out for me: 'He wrote some decent short stories, but I saw him recently returning from an international literary festival or whatever wearing a baseball cap with the name of a gin on it and a T-shirt bearing another brand name. He does this lecture thing about the martini in literature. It's rather sad, really.'

But I asked her more questions about our school days. 'I know that you have little interest these days in our past, and do not "dwell on it" as you say. I find I am still writing about it. Nothing ever concludes. I don't know whether I told you I went back to our high school and read the chapter "Portrait of a Virgin Girl" from *Forty-Seventeen*, which I know you haven't read. No response from the students. But I felt all sorts of interactions and emotions . . . Oddly, throughout my life I've dreamt of you just about every week. My therapist says not to worry about it . . . Do you remember a friend of my mother's telling you when we were married that my mother wanted a girl when I was born? At my mother's funeral she told me that again. What was she trying to tell us? Me?'

Margaret replied: 'Obviously I haven't forgotten our past (though some bits are blurred). I think you must have been very brave to go back to the old school and read what you've written to the students of Today.

'People's memories differ so much, don't they? I'm not sure how much we can trust them at all. When I got together with my sisters and brother last year it was quite obvious that all their memories differed from mine, and when June did her oration at Mum's funeral it all sounded terrific but the facts, according to my knowledge, were entirely up the creek . . .

'About dreaming: I'm sure your therapist is absolutely right. You're in my dreams too (but not so frequently). You often appear in them but your presence is not threatening in any way. I imagine it is because of all those formative years together so I am not disturbed by the dreams. I'm a big dreamer, with lots of complications and intricacies!

'About the other matter you mentioned, it would make sense that your mother would want a girl after having two sons, but unless she dressed you in pink and allowed your hair to grow into long girlish curls, her unrealised wish should not have affected you.

'Over here, things are not going too badly for us and the weather is being uncommonly benign which is a bonus . . .

'Love Margaret.'

End Pieces

A LETTER TO MY DRINKING COMPANIONS AROUND THE WORLD

This memoir is not a comprehensive overview of my life or my relationships and is not meant, therefore, as a complete diagram of my life now or in the past. It is, in the main, a ruminative set of memories and ideas triggered by a consideration of the martini and its folklore. Nothing more or less. It is, in a way, a commonplace book of personal notes, a project of connoisseurship and folklore. And as I look back, surprisingly, a small project of self-reconciliation.

To my friends I feel I need to say that the absence of your name or the number of times you are mentioned is not necessarily in any way an indication of where you fit into my life or how much I care for you. In the writing of the book there was no consideration or calculation of proportion or fairness in terms of affection. It was the subterranean logic which determined where the book went and who was consequently mentioned. Some of you do not even drink martinis. Some of you do not even drink!

It is, in passing, also a consideration of the relationship of fiction to memory and to the writer's life and it begins with the unpacking of an earlier story of mine entitled 'Martini' – the making of stories from stories, I suppose, and how stories can bubble out from other stories.

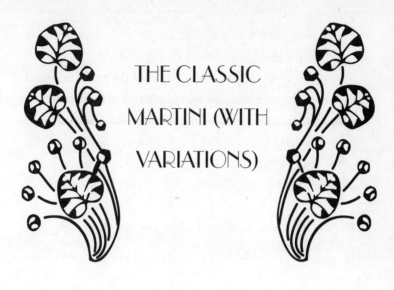

THE CLASSIC MARTINI (WITH VARIATIONS)

FIRST VARIATION
6 parts London gin
1 part dry vermouth

Place ingredients in a chilled cocktail shaker filled with ice.

Cover and shake to the rhythm of a waltz.

When contents are icy cold, strain and pour to the brim of a chilled martini glass.

Garnish with a green olive on the end of a wooden toothpick.

The olive may be unpitted or stuffed with pimento. Up to three olives may be used.

The toothpick should be rounded and wooden, sharpened at one end, with a small groove near the blunt end.

The olive and toothpick may be replaced by a twist of lemon rind, which may be sculpted into a bow, a spiral or a snake.

SECOND VARIATION
Place vermouth into a chilled cocktail shaker filled with ice.

Cover and shake, then discard excess vermouth, leaving only the vermouth-coated ice cubes.

Add gin, cover and shake to the rhythm of a waltz.

Proceed according to the First Variation.

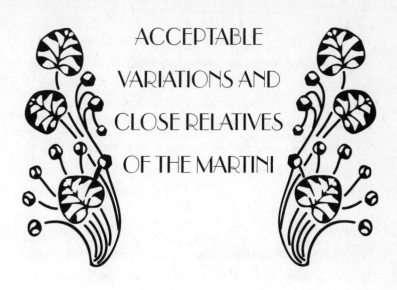

ACCEPTABLE VARIATIONS AND CLOSE RELATIVES OF THE MARTINI

THE VODKA OR KANGAROO

Made according to the two classic martini variations, with vodka replacing the gin. Because there are usually no herbs, spices or other botanicals in vodka, the martini made with it is less complex. I have heard the vodka martini described as a 'kangaroo' in New York.

THE JACK LONDON

'50:50 gin and dry vermouth were thought to be the proportions of the martini when it started, probably in Europe, or in any place where London gin and Italian or French vermouth were available and the drinkers adventurous.'

THE GIN TURIN

Gin, dry and sweet vermouth 50:25:25. A Genevan forerunner of the martini, drunk by the *bon viveurs* of the 1920s.

THE VODKA TURIN
Vodka, dry and sweet vermouth 50:25:25. As drunk by Mary McGeachy.

THE VOLTZ PEDANTIC
A classic in which the gin and vermouth are individually shaken in ice and separate cocktail shakers then combined and mixed in a third shaker.

THE RODMAN
Named after connoisseur and script writer Howard A. Rodman (*Joe Gould's Secret, Charley Varrick, Coogan's Bluff, Madigan*). 'The day before your guests arrive, put all the ingredients – glasses, gin, and shaker – in the refrigerator. Use a thermometer to make sure the ice is about twenty degrees below zero (centigrade). Don't take anything out until your friends arrive; then pour a few drops of Noilly Prat and half a demitasse spoon of Angostura bitters over the ice in the shaker. Shake it, then pour the liquid out, leaving only the ice, which retains a faint taste of both. Then pour straight gin over the ice in the shaker, shake it again, and serve.' Rodman believes each person's martini should be mixed separately.

THE MALCOLM FRASER
'Malcolm Fraser is said to take a swig of gin from the bottle, swallow it, and then pour in some vermouth to replace the gin. He shakes the bottle and then places it in the freezer for martinis when required.'

THE ALGONQUIN TRADITIONAL

The classic in proportions of 3 parts gin 1 part vermouth, with a spot of orange bitters all mixed and served very cold in cobalt-blue martini glasses. Also known as the Dorothy Parker.

THE ALGONQUIN DIAMOND

The hotel offers a $10,000 martini, complete with a loose diamond at the bottom.

THE BON

The Sydney Writers' Week official cocktail, 2005 – the Algonquin Traditional without the orange bitters. Called the BON martini by Jessie Dettmann of Random House to indicate that this book would be Out in November.

THE OGDEN NASH YELLOW MELLOW

'Voltz and I discovered that the yellow mellow martini is reached by adding .12 vermouths to every one part of gin.'

THE CONTEMPORARY

'Today most bars, unless instructed otherwise, serve a severely dry martini from which the vermouth is all but excluded. Most bartenders will swirl vermouth in the glass, throw it away and then serve chilled gin or vodka with an olive or two or three or a twist, often sculpted, sometimes into a bow, a spiral, a snake.'

Another name for the second variation of the classic.

THE MONTGOMERY
'Hemingway mentions what he calls the Montgomery martini in his novel *Across the River and into the Trees*. A Montgomery is gin and vermouth in proportions of 15:1 — the name is a reference to the English World War II Field Marshal General Montgomery who, legend has it, would not attack without overwhelming superiority.'

THE QUEEN MOTHER
'Eleven to one, please.' The Queen Mother was known to love the martini.

THE WET MARTINI
Heavy on the vermouth. 'The other day I ordered a martini the way I sometimes like it: 5 parts gin to 1 part vermouth (which would be the way the *New Yorker* crowd would have drunk it in the 1930s), and the young woman bartender queried this and said, "You want a wet martini, not a dry martini?" I hadn't heard this expression and I asked her about it. She said she'd picked it up in London.'

THE DIRTY MARTINI
Preferred quantites of gin and dry vermouth.
Olive brine — flick, splash or dash (see page 90)

Place ingredients in a chilled cocktail shaker filled with ice.

Cover and shake to the rhythm of a waltz.

When contents are icy cold, strain and pour to the brim of a chilled martini glass.

Garnish with green olive(s) on the end of a wooden toothpick.

'"Often when olives are added to martinis, a little brine from the olive jar gets into the drink from the olives, sometimes more than at other times. Someone, somewhere decided to call it a dirty martini and to intentionally put a little more brine than would normally come off the olives."'

THE ROOSEVELT
The favourite martini of the former president of the United States, Franklin Roosevelt. Two parts gin, one part vermouth, a splash of olive brine and possibly a dot or two of orange bitters.

GIN & IT
2:1 gin and sweet vermouth.

THE ABSINTHE
'... the manservant brought in a tray with an array of bottles and Isabel, always tactful, knowing that nine men out of ten are convinced they can mix a better cocktail than any woman, asked me to shake a couple. I poured out the gin and the Noilly Prat and added the dash of absinthe that transforms a dry Martini from a nondescript drink to one for the gods of Olympus . . .'

W. Somerset Maugham, *The Fall of Edward Bannard*, 1921

A classic gin martini with a dash of absinthe added to the glass before pouring the martini.

THE STUART
'In 1896, the New York barman Thomas Stuart published *Stuart's Fancy Drinks and How to Make Them*, which has a recipe for what he called the Marquerite but which resembles what we know as a martini: 2 parts Plymouth gin, 1 part French vermouth with a dot or two of orange bitters.'

THE ORANGE BITTERS MARTINI
A classic martini with one or a few dots of orange bitters added to the shaker. Fee Brothers recommend one to three dashes. This is arguably the martini drunk in the US of the 1930s/1940s/1950s (see The Stuart).

THE HONGELL
A classic martini served in a Hongell glass, that is wide at the rim and then narrows down slightly to a heavy heel or base with no stem.

THE GIBSON
A close relative of the martini.

A classic martini served with a pickled onion instead of an olive and also mixed to the rhythm of the waltz. 'It was named after a pen-and-ink illustrator for the American magazine *Life*, Charles Dana Gibson, who died in 1940.'

THE MANHATTAN

A distant relative of the martini. 1 part whisky to $\frac{1}{4}$ part sweet vermouth, with a dash of bitters, served in a martini glass. Variations are made with dry vermouth and combinations of sweet and dry vermouth, shaken to the rhythm of a foxtrot.

THE DESERT WIND

Charles Willeford writes, in *Wild Wives*: 'I call my martini a Desert Wind. Nine-tenths gin, one-tenth vermouth. No olive. No onion. Nothing. Just a toothpick.'

THE HARRY CATTERNS

'When I was living with Sarah Ducker and her son Harry, who was about six, he would enjoy mixing the martinis at the cocktail hour. He would have a juice and I would have a martini while we watched the television news. During one mixing he misremembered my instructions and put the olives in the martini shaker rather than the glass. After he had finished his mixing, we fished them out of the cocktail shaker and put them in my martini glass. It was, accidentally, an acceptable innovation to the martini. From then on we called this martini a "Harry Catterns" . . .'

THE OLDER MAN

In the chapter from *Forty-Seventeen* entitled 'Martini', the older man says that now he is approaching the age of forty, he prefers his martini 5:1 with an olive, very cold.

THE NAKED MARTINI
Only vodka or gin and an olive – no vermouth.

THE GIMLET
A distant relative from the 1920s. 2$^{1}/_{2}$ parts gin, to $^{3}/_{4}$ fresh lime juice – or, at a pinch, Rose's bottled lime juice – served in a martini glass with a wedge of lime as garnish.

THE VESUVIO
A mad relative. Equal parts gin and vodka, no vermouth.

> . . . our *Vesuvio* martinis
> with no vermouth but vodka
> to sweeten the dry gin –

Also drunk by Ian Fleming.

THE JAMES BOND
'. . . three measures of Gordon's, one of vodka, half a measure of Kina Lillet. Shake it very well until it's ice-cold, then add lemon peel.' From *Casino Royale*.

Lillet Blanc is a French aperitif white wine – close to being a vermouth – with a taste of citrus. It is usually served chilled with a slice of orange, either on its own or with ice. It is the favourite drink of Hannibal Lecter from *Silence of the Lambs*.

THE SQUIRREL

A classic martini with an acorn instead of an olive.

Served only to squirrels.

THE UPSIDE DOWN

'Roger Angell in an essay in the *New Yorker* on the martini says he has a sister-in-law who likes what he calls an upside-down martini — a martini with the usual proportions reversed — that is, a drink which is mostly vermouth with a little gin.'

(Sunni, the much loved waiter at the Bayswater Brasserie, often suggests an upside-down martini, and laughs.)

THE VIRGIN

'A woman told me that when she felt like a martini but didn't feel like drinking she'd make a shaker of ice and water with just a dash of gin, a taste of vermouth — enough to give the drink a suggestion of the martini — and add a twist. "I drink these sometimes while reading," she said, "and while dreaming of a martini".'

THE TIN HOUSE

Designed for the NY magazine *Tin House* by Greg Connolly, bartender at the Four Seasons restaurant in NYC.

Pour $\frac{1}{2}$ part of Pernod into a cocktail shaker and swirl until it coats the inside of the shaker, pour off the liquid. Absinthe can be substituted for pernod. Splash 2 eye-dropperfuls of dry vermouth into the bottom of the shaker and again swirl it and then pour off the liquid.

Pour 4 to $4\frac{1}{2}$ parts of Tanqueray gin into the shaker, add ice, and with a ridiculously long-handled silver mixing spoon stir twenty times (exactly).

Pour the drink into a very well-chilled martini glass and then add three small green olives, or two large ones, without a toothpick.

One of these olives should be eaten only after the martini has been drunk.

ON THE ROCKS

Any of the above versions served in a large martini glass with ice, preferably in chips with Sharon Stone edges, served in a large martini glass.

THE BLACK THORN FAUX MARTINI

$1\frac{1}{2}$ parts sloe gin to 1 part sweet vermouth, shaken in a cocktail shaker with ice, served in a chilled martini glass garnished with a twist of lemon. This drink only sounds like a martini.

Crazy drinks

THE FLIRTINI

Raspberry syrup, 1 part 'Razberi' flavoured Stolichnaya vodka, 1 part Cointreau, lime, pineapple and cranberry juices, and a splash of champagne served in a martini glass. Sarah Jessica Parker named it the Flirtini.

THE COSMOPOLITAN (SOMETIMES CALLED A PINK MARTINI)

$1^1/_2$ parts vodka, 1 part Cointreau, $^1/_2$ part lime and 1 part cranberry juice – a good drink in itself but not a relative of the martini.

ESPRESSO CHOCOLATE MARTINI

1 cold espresso coffee: $1^1/_2$ vodka: $1^1/_2$ coffee liqueur: 1 Crème de Cacao.

TIMES SQUARE TOOTSIE

1:1 Godiva chocolate liqueur and Cointreau (garnish, a slice of orange).

Tootsie is slang for a woman and the name of the 1982 film in which Dustin Hoffman crossdresses.

THE SIDECAR

2 parts brandy

1 part lemon juice

1 part Cointreau

Rim glass with coarse granulated sugar. Combine in cocktail shaker with ice, shake well, strain and pour into glass with a sugar cube.

One of the drinks of Scott and Zelda Fitzgerald.

MARTINI
MUSIC

Old songs are more than tunes,
They are little houses in which our hearts once lived.

Ben Hecht

The music I like to drink with is described in an advertisement
for a CD called *Cocktail Piano Music*, put together by Jim Haskins.
Haskins says, 'Cocktail piano music . . . is quiet, sophisticated
music, not quite jazz and not quite classical, but drawing from
both schools. It usually features the great standards of the 3os
and 4os from such gifted writers as George Gershwin, Harold
Arlen, Duke Ellington, Rodgers & Hart and many others. It is
music to end your day with . . . In short, you're about to make a
new friend . . .'

Haskins includes these tunes in his selection: These Foolish
Things, Fly Me to the Moon, Stormy Weather, Misty, Here's
That Rainy Day, April in Paris, I Let a Song Out of My Heart,

September Song, Laura, As Time Goes By, I See Your Face
Before Me, I Guess I'll Have to Change My Plan, Dancing On
the Ceiling, Time After Time, Georgia On My Mind, Long Ago
and Far Away, All the Things You Are, Ramona, Tenderly, Emily,
Stars Fell On Alabama, Nobody's Heart, You Are Too Beautiful,
Come Rain or Come Shine, Satin Doll, I Loves You Porgy, Bless
You Is My Woman, Angel Eyes, He Loves and She Loves, Remind
Me, It's the Talk of the Town, While We're Young, Cry Me a
River, I Get Along Without You Very Well.

But you have to have Billie Holiday: Wished on the Moon,
What a Little Moonlight Can Do, Miss Brown to You, Sunbonnet
Blue (And a Little Straw Hat), I Cried for You, Summertime,
Billie's Blues, Fine Romance, Let's Call a Heart a Heart, Easy to
Love, Way You Look Tonight, Who Loves You?, Pennies From
Heaven, Carelessly, Let's Call the Whole Thing Off, They Can't
Take That Away From Me, I'll Get By (As Long as I Have You),
Mean to Me, Easy Living, I'll Never be the Same, Me, Myself and
I, He's Funny That Way, Nice Work If You Can Get It, My Man,
Can't Help Lovin' Dat Man, I Can't Believe That You're in Love
With Me, You Go to My Head.

Or Jackie Gleason's suggestions from 'Music, Martinis and
Memories' (1955): I Got It Bad and That Ain't Good, My Ideal,
I Remember You, Shangri-la, It Could Happen to You, Somebody
Loves Me, The Song is Ended, Once in a While, I Can't Get
Started, Yesterdays, I'll be Seeing You, Time On My Hands.

And I would add Cole Porter's Miss Otis Regrets, Anything
Goes, What is This Thing Called Love, Night and Day, Let's
Misbehave, Please Don't Make Me Be Good. And always, always,
Moon River.

WHAT IS THIS DEMON?
ALCOHOL AND
THE ART OF
DRINKING

Explaining alcohol is a bit like trying to explain electricity to a private school student.

What we drink is ethyl alcohol, known as ethanol, a clear, thin, odourless liquid – essentially a neutral liquid (the word *alcohol* comes from Arabic *al-kuhul*, yeah right, whatever you say, Mr Lexicographer) and originally referred to any *essence* of any substance (including powders) brought about by refining or distilling and from there the word moved to describe the liquid products of distillation or refinement, and this led to our current usage, that is, an intoxicating liquid.

Alcohol is produced by *fermentation*, which occurs naturally when yeast, a microscopic plant (found in many places if you know where to look), is mixed with the sugar in fruit or vegetable juice. The process stops naturally when about 14% of the juice has turned to alcohol. Mead, made from honey, is thought to be the oldest recorded alcoholic drink but I would suspect that many cultures stumbled onto it at around the same time in its many natural manifestations – rotting fruit, grapes and so on. Alcohol can form naturally in fruit and in the sap of trees and very early in our history humans discovered this natural alcohol and began using it for pleasure and ritual.

The traditional flavours of alcoholic drinks come indirectly from the plants from which the alcohol is made – grapes, grains, fruits and so on – and while the original flavours themselves may not survive the process (wine doesn't really taste of grapes and nor does vodka taste of potatoes) the new flavours which do emerge have determined the classification, lore and mythologies of the various drinks.

Distillation is the process used to make beverages with a higher alcohol content than the natural 14%. We humans just can't leave well enough alone. In this process the fermented liquid is heated until it vaporises and the water content is reduced and the alcohol content increased. That is what happens in all those curling tubes on home-made stills. Distilled alcoholic beverages – whisky, gin, vodka and rum and so on – are referred to as spirits and usually contain 40% to 50% alcohol although are sometimes much higher.

When drinking an alcoholic drink some of the alcohol is absorbed through the stomach walls into the bloodstream but most passes into the small intestine and then into the blood-stream. It circulates through the body tissue and to the brain and within about ten to twenty minutes the drinker begins to feel its effects.

A large person does not feel the effects of a drink as quickly as a small person because large people have more blood in their bodies in which the alcohol is diluted.

A woman is likely to feel the effects of alcohol sooner than a man because it brings about rapid changes in the testosterone levels in the woman and because men are statistically larger than women. Because of its hormonal affect, a woman the same size as a man will show a higher alcohol level after the same number of drinks.

The body disposes of alcohol in two ways: elimination and oxidation. Only about 10% of the alcohol in the body leaves through being burned as energy and then eliminated from the lungs as gas. Some leaves the body through the kidneys as urine. About 90% of the alcohol leaves the body by oxidation through the liver. The liver oxidises the alcohol and excretes it into the bile.

Bile is a fluid containing water, electrolytes and bile acids. The alcohol along with other stuff flows through the biliary tract into the small intestine from where it is eliminated from the body as faeces. The liver can oxidise about one drink every hour – which is why the morning after a heavy night you may find, if breathtested, that you still have alcohol in your body. The body recovers from alcohol faster than the brain. Walking around the block might burn off one drink. Coffee does not reduce the alcohol in your body or its physical effects, but the caffeine may brighten you up.

Some drinks have more alcohol in them than others. Beer usually has between 2% and 6% alcohol, table wines from 11% to 14%, fortified or dessert wines (such as sherry or port) have

16% to 20%, and distilled spirits usually range from 40% to 50%.

A regular glass of beer, a standard wine glass of wine or a measured nip of spirits have evolved traditionally and legally to contain approximately the same amount of alcohol per drink – so that we know where we are. Cocktails such as the martini break from the standard measures and become drinks of unknown potency – hence their mystery.

A person who has a drink after eating a meal will feel less effect because the food slows the absorption of the alcohol, and can also carry some of it out of the system. A person with an 'empty stomach' will absorb the alcohol faster.

The risky alcohol level is 1% in the blood, at which the breathing becomes paralysed and death occurs. However this is a very difficult level to achieve – usually we pass out or are sick before we can achieve this (although God knows, some of us try). Drinking yourself to death in this way is not really possible although when I was at high school one of my friends had a girlfriend who drank a whole bottle of gin on the beach and died.

Alcohol affects the central nervous system but not the muscles or the senses themselves, only the *control* of these muscles and senses.

Depending on the amount, alcohol can be a mild tranquilliser or can work as a general anaesthetic, albeit a poor one – pity those cowboys we see in movies who drink a bottle of whisky before their legs are amputated with a rusty saw.

Dr Linda Calabresi, a practising GP and medical editor of *Medical Observer* and health columnist says this: 'It is a popular myth that alcohol destroys brain cells – but untrue. Alcohol is a depressant slowing the activity of nerve cells in the brain. It affects all areas of the brain, including the frontal lobe, causing loss of reason and inhibition; parietal lobe, leading to loss of fine motor skills and slower reaction times; temporal lobe, giving slurred speech; occipital lobe, causing blurred vision and poor distance judgement; and the cerebellum, leading to lack of co-ordination and balance. Having said that, these effects are rarely permanent. Permanent brain damage is usually confined to long-term heavy alcohol users. There have been studies that show a moderate consumption of alcohol (one to two drinks a day) is associated with improved mental ability.'

Some studies show that we become considerably more physically attractive to the person we are drinking with.

Why do we become dehydrated when we drink alcohol – with all that fluid going into our bodies? The alcohol causes us to discharge more fluid than we take in.

Luxembourg and Hungary consume the most alcohol per person – over ten litres per head – with Australia at about eight litres, slightly ahead of the US which is around six litres. France is around ten litres per head.

These days, we undertake drastic changes to our diet in search of mystical rejuvenation of our body, or as a renewal of our personality, or to attain longevity (though the more I see of debilitated old age the less attractive longevity becomes). The promulgation of these changes of diet to friends and relatives usually says, 'I am about to become a profoundly different person – if you want to stay up with me, you had better change as well'. Many diets carry a prohibitive attitude to alcohol. The timorous mineral water and the 'better not' attitude to life rather than the 'why not?' attitude seem to me to be among the saddest of the health postures – a loss of joy, hedonism and self-exploration.

The anti-alcohol hysteria seems worse among the intelligentsia of the US. I came across a miserable example in the *New Yorker*. A journalist unthinkingly writes that the rock singer Jerry Garcia and he 'had some Chinese food cooked without any oil and, to prevent an overdose of health, some good champagne'.

Cooking with some oils is not bad for your health, Chinese food is one of the healthiest, and, for God's sake, a glass of champagne is not 'anti-health' by any medical measure.

I do not want to put pressure on people who shouldn't drink alcohol and I acknowledge that there are such people. And some people find alcohol an unpleasant drink. Abuse of alcohol does lead to health problems.

I also acknowledge that some people are always at ease, socially brilliant, articulate and playful without a drink. Maybe I speak for the less than socially adequate.

I write more to counter the damage the new prohibitions do to the art of dining and to some of our finer social traditions of celebration and fellowship. I mean the implied bond which is inherent in drinking alcohol with someone, the bond of shared angst, the implicit offering of candour (not always forthcoming), the act of simple companionship, even if that companionship is only that of the night.

And yes, the shared drinks do involve a subtle social risk of self-exposure, of the slackening of the formal and disciplined self. It is a little adventure.

To be blunt, I think that the world would be a better place if more people took a few drinks now and then. As Humphrey Bogart said, 'The problem with the world is that everyone is a few drinks behind.'

I want at this point to say that I also continue to defend occasional deep intoxication. It is not for everyone. Not for every day. But it has its wonders.

It has also to be said, however, that it took me nearly a lifetime to learn that one could drink just one or two glasses, say with food, and then stop drinking and go on to other activities without the accompaniment of alcohol.

I also concede that alcohol enhances very few activities, not surgery or driving or flying, but conversation and dining are the obvious ones that it does enhance.

I have also observed people who improve intellectually after a few drinks. Alcohol seems to bring clarity and releases vocabulary in some people; removes intellectual shyness. It sponsors daring connections that they would not have otherwise made.

Timothy Mo in his novel *The Redundancy of Courage* observes that the Canadian woman journalist 'would put back a very large highball and seem to become only more focused'.

Creative work and important decisions in my experience benefit from being discussed both in the sober condition *and* after a few drinks.

The adage about drink that 'it makes old friends seem like new friends and new friends seem like old friends' is a perfect description of the beneficial effects of alcohol in creating a renewed awareness of each other and contributing to the art of listening (not always).

As for jet lag and drinking, I have flown quite a lot and have sometimes taken drinks and sometimes not, and I think the connection between alcohol and jet lag is nonsense. Long flights across time zones are inescapably disorienting. Putting brown paper in the soles of your shoes doesn't work either. Travel is often *enhanced* by a few drinks, especially the plane trip and the train journey, but also the arrival.

And some of my finest musing has been done at a solitary meal in a restaurant, with a book or a magazine and a bottle of wine; alcohol then becomes the ring master of my mental circus.

I can't help but think that for some people the health hysteria does mask a revived puritanism: the fear of the unvisited self; and the search for ever more control of self through diet; the conviction that one doesn't deserve easy pleasure or any pleasure but also, and much worse, the disapproval of other people's pleasure.

Allow me to quote a couple of my own beloved characters, Edith and Ambrose, from *Grand Days* and *Dark Palace*.

Ambrose tells Edith his precepts about drinking, including precept six which is: To drink too quickly is unpleasant; to drink too much is a waste.

Edith replies, 'I think I have a new precept and it contains a saving grace.'

'What is this new precept?'

'That everyone who has taken drink becomes a little mad.'

'A very good observation. But where is the saving grace?'

'The saving grace is that as long as everyone in the circle is drinking, the madness is shared, and therefore may not seem to be madness to those in that circle. What would be misbehaviour for a non-drinker is – among those drinking – forgiven or passes unnoticed. And on many occasions, never remembered, or if remembered, is excused.'

Edith also learns that people remember their *own* embarrassments and rarely those of others.

The spacing of the drinks is required if both the drink and the cadence of intoxication is to be appreciated, allowing us to feel the drink in our body and in our consciousness. Spacing avoids the blind, blurred, insensate rush to oblivion.

It has to be admitted that sometimes, in dark times, I am inclined to the blind, blurred, insensate rush to oblivion. Well, perhaps never quite insensate. I once quoted Chekhov to Voltz. Vanya, in the play *Uncle Vanya*, says, 'I drink to create the illusion that I might be alive.'

'Sometimes I think Chekhov was a Martian,' Voltz said. 'His emotional response to the world was profound – but profoundly and inevitably wrong. Nobody drinks to remind himself that he's alive. You drink to get the hell out of here.' It was the only time that I have known Voltz to swear.

I have discussed the Japanese tea ceremony and its relationship to martini drinking. Neither the Japanese tea ceremony nor martini drinking have an expression to des-cribe the condition of feeling angst and finding that intoxication simply changes the nature of the angst. But we all know it does.

The drinking rules of my youth were: don't drink before midday; don't mix your drinks; don't drink on an empty stomach; don't mix grape and grain; do not begin your drinking before your companions; and if you avoid drinking spirits you will avoid becoming an alcoholic.

In my experience, only 'not drinking on an empty stomach' has any validity and not starting drinking before your companions is good form. And I think it is good to remember the golden rule of the British Foreign Office: never to be drunk at the wrong time of the day. That is probably related to not drinking before midday, however it is sometimes a guilty pleasure to do just that.

Sculptured drinking requires the spacing of drinks — sometimes called pacing oneself — which requires the selection of the appropriate drinks to the time of day and to the season and in relation to meals (see martinis at breakfast), the appropriate glass, the combination of atmosphere, light, music, company or reading matter (itself a form of company), view (water, cityscape, parkland) or non-view (in a shuttered bar facing the wall, never facing a mirror), and angst with which to engender a comfortable what-the-hell mood. It is sometimes possible to at least attempt to savour the absurdity of finding oneself a conflicted person with no way out.

But don't dwell too long on the unfairness of it. Being unconflicted has a downside too.

NOTES

FROM 'THE VENERATED CRAFT' AND 'THEY HAD A DATE WITH FATE IN CASABLANCA'

The Thin Man films (there were five) were based on novels by Dashiell Hammett (1894–1961) who also wrote *The Maltese Falcon*. Hammett's books have now become part of the Library of Congress American classics series.

He was a long time companion of writer Lillian Hellman (1905–1984).

The blurb of my copy of *The Thin Man* says, 'Nick and Nora Charles are Dashiell Hammett's most enchanting creations, a rich, glamorous couple who solve homicides in between wisecracks and martinis.'

Curiously enough, the blurb writer is totally wrong. The martini cocktail is never mentioned in the book. It is as if the blurb writer wanted the characters to drink martinis – or, more likely, that the blurb writer had seen the film but not read the book.

Hammett and his characters were Scotch and soda drinkers. Legend has it that Hammett himself drank 'like he had no expectation of being alive much beyond Thursday'.

I sent this information to Voltz.

He replied, 'It may be of interest to you to know that Hammett died on a Tuesday.'

One critic has described Hammett as one of those writers who lifted detective fiction into an intelligent literary genre with the hypotheses that human society is driven by greed, brutality, and treachery – Voltz's view of life.

Hammett went to gaol in the 1950s for refusing to give evidence to the House Un-American Activities Committee set up to investigate communist influence in the US.

Both he and Hellman were involved in leftist activities and organisations, however Hellman said that she never joined the Communist Party although she was certainly slow to condemn it.

In 1952 Hellman was called to appear before HUAC but instead she fled from the US. In a famous letter to the committee refusing to reveal the names of associates and friends who might have communist associations, she wrote: 'But to hurt innocent people whom I knew many years ago in order to save myself is, to me, inhuman and indecent and dishonourable. I cannot and will not cut my conscience to fit this year's fashions, even though I long ago came to the conclusion that I was not a political person and could have no comfortable place in any political group . . .'

Hellman and Hammett were both blacklisted by Hollywood from the late 1940s to the 1960s.

FROM 'THE DIAMOND: THE PEARL: THE ACORN'
Pliny tells a version of the Cleopatra's pearl story in his *Natural History* (IX.59.119–121) as does Horace in *Satires* (II.3.239).

FROM 'THE WHOLE QUESTION OF THE DRINKS' CART'
The Second World War began shortly after Susan Kozma completed the Schreibers' living room. The Schreibers fled to London, taking some possessions with them including the drinks' trolley. The Victoria and Albert Museum eventually found the drinks' trolley and acquired it for their collection.

The V and A also has Ernest Race's *Bottleship Mark II* (1963) which is a combined drinks' cupboard and magazine rack on wheels. Race is best known for his Penguin Donkey: a strange two-sided bookcase designed to house only Penguin books.

FROM 'WHERE ARE THEY NOW?'
Inaccrochable.
Gertrude Stein, when talking to Hemingway about one of his short stories said, 'It's good. That's not the question at all. But it is *inaccrochable*. That means it is like a picture that a painter paints and then he cannot hang it when he has a show.'

'But what if it is not dirty but it is only that you are trying to use words that people would actually use. That are the only words that can make the story come true and that you must use them? You have to use them?'

From Hemingway's *A Moveable Feast*.

SOURCES

Medical details in this book when not attributed are taken from standard sources such as the Merck manuals or from medically trained drinkers including Dr John Marsden and his BBC program on alcohol.

Some extracts of this book were previously published in different versions: 'Memoir of a Story: Story of a Memoir' in *Best Australian Stories 2003*; 'Meeting Mary McGeachy' appeared as 'Martini Festival' in *The Sydney Morning Herald*'s 'Spectrum'; 'Martini City' appeared in a different form in *The Good Weekend*; a version of 'Martini – the story' appeared as 'Martini', a chapter from *Forty-Seventeen* (1988); the chairperson piece on toothpicks is from my book *Lateshows* (1990).

Two names have been changed to avoid embarrassment to living people.

p.3o   The description of Tennessee Williams' typical writing day comes from Dotson Rader, *Tennessee: Cry of the Heart* (1985)

p.33   My friend Michael Fraser told me that he had lost a girl-friend once when he asked her whether he could 'fix her a drink'

p.35   The Toronto Study is by C. C. Trevithick, research assistant, M. M. Chartrand, research assistant, J. Wahlman, research assistant, F. Rahman, research assistant, M. Hirst, professor, J. R. Trevithick, professor, from the Department of Biochemistry, Faculty of Medicine and Dentistry, University of Western Ontario, Canada

p.42   The argument for having a very small amount of melting ice water in a martini comes from Robert Hess's website 'Drinkboy' (www.drinkboy.com)

p.43   Howard A. Rodman's advice about ice comes from an email he sent to Steven Katz, forwarded to me with permission

p.47   My martini-drinking writer friend in Paris is Tim Baker

p.49   'Fire and Ice' from *The Poetry of Robert Frost*, edited by Edward Connery Lathem. Copyright 1923, 1969 by Henry Holt and Company. Copyright 1951 by Robert Frost. Reprinted by permission of Henry Holt and Company, LLC

p.56   Robert Lowell's 'Homecoming' is from *Collected Poems*, edited by Frank Bidart and David Gewanter (2003) p.65 The information about the wet martini comes from a conversation with Alison Handley

p.66 Ogden Nash, 'A Drink with Something in It' (1935)

p.69 Somerset Maugham, *The Fall of Edward Bannard* (1921)

p.77 The adjective 'modernist' and 'moderne' (from the Latin word *modo* meaning 'just now') is applied to the martini and its glass by Max Rudin in an essay 'There is Something About a Martini'(*American Heritage* magazine, July–August 1997)

p.85 The art of cocking the tail comes from an email sent to me by Virginia Gordon

p.95 Kurt Vonnegut Jnr, *Breakfast of Champions* (1973)

p.120 G.K. Chesterton, 'A Ballade of an Anti-Puritan' in *Poems* (1915)

p.128 F. Scott Fitzgerald, *The Great Gatsby* (1925)

p.129 'Moonlight Cocktail', Glenn Miller and his Orchestra. Words by Kim Gannon. Music by Lucky Roberts

p.141 The information about autotrays comes from Susan Butler p.145   Susan Kozma was not well when I talked with her. This is a constructed version of her remarks, given coherence from other sources, but it is, I know, the gist of her thinking

p.160   The quote from Jean Rhys comes from *The Left Bank* (1927)

p.169   The Sadness of Evanescence: the idea of the martini always being in a transitory state comes from Sandra Forbes

OTHER SOURCES INCLUDE:
Barnaby Conrad III, *The Martini* (1995)

Harry Craddock, *The Savoy Cocktail Book* (reprinted 1999)

John Doxat, *World of Drinks and Drinking* (1971) and private correspondence between the author and Doxat

Lowell Edmunds, *Martini, Straight Up: The Classic American Cocktail* (1998)

William Grimes, *Cultural History of the Cocktail* (1993)

Catherine Gilbert Murdock, *Domesticating Drink: Women, Men, and Alcohol in America, 1870–1940* (1998)

ACKNOWLEDGMENTS

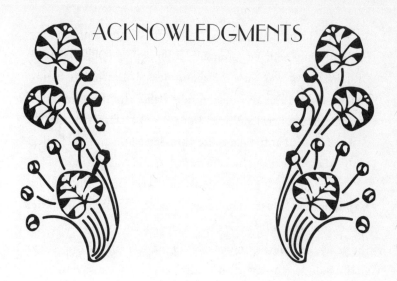

There is a special thanks due to two great sports, Steven Katz (screenwriter of *Shadow of a Vampire*) who has been an assiduous investigator of the martini over the years, and a great martini companion; and to Matt Condon, companion and informant, who is not a martini drinker.

Other friends and good sports who gave me wisdom for this book were Don Anderson, Xavier Hennekinne, Judy Rymer, Jane Palfreyman, Virginia Gordon, David Catterns, Robert Taylor, Tim Herbert, Wendy Dear, Michael Fraser, Harry Catterns, Michele Garnaut, Barry and Jenny Porter, Lenore Coltheart, Joanna Logue, Annie Coulthard, Julia Leigh, Ophelia and Michele Field, Derek Johns, Sam Dettmann and Sam Gerovich.

And thanks to THE MARTINI WORKSHOP, run by Susie Carleton, Verity and Xavier, those other fine elves who joined with me to explore the history of the drink: Annette Hughes, Annie Coulthard, Peter Banki, Angela Bowne, Brian and

Suzanne Kiernan, David Kirk, Catharine Lumby, Duncan Fine, Caroline Bucknell, Ed Campion, Patsi Zeppel, Don and Betsy Graham, Carol and Nick Dettmann, Jessica Dettmann, Sandra Forbes, Robert Farrar, Tim and Julie Baker, Jim Freston, Rosemary Creswell, Errol Sullivan, Donald and Myfanwy Horne.

The bar staff at the Bayswater Brasserie are almost a College of the Martini, especially Leonard Opai and Naren Young.

The final draft of this book was written at the historic Minnamurra House, Jamberoo, owned by Carol and Nick Dettmann, and offered to me so generously for my work over the years; and in the home of Roscrana and Parkes Chrestman in the Blue Mountains, also kindly loaned to me as a retreat.

I thank Meredith Sime and Susie Carleton and the University of New South Wales, who were patrons of this book.

I want to especially thank Don Anderson, Angela Bowne, Xavier Hennekinne, Matt Condon, Johanna Baldwin, Jane Cameron, and Tim Herbert for reading the manuscript and offering incisive responses. Thanks to Jessica Dettmann for coming up with the line 'How to live a martini and mix a life'. And thank you to my agents, Lesley McFadzean and Siobhan Hannan.

A extra-special thanks to Jane Palfreyman, my publisher, for being so accommodating and so inspiring of such an eccentric book.

And of course, as ever, my very special thanks to my dear friend and former agent over many years, Rosemary Creswell, who was never fazed by the messes I got myself into around the world and to whom this book is dedicated.

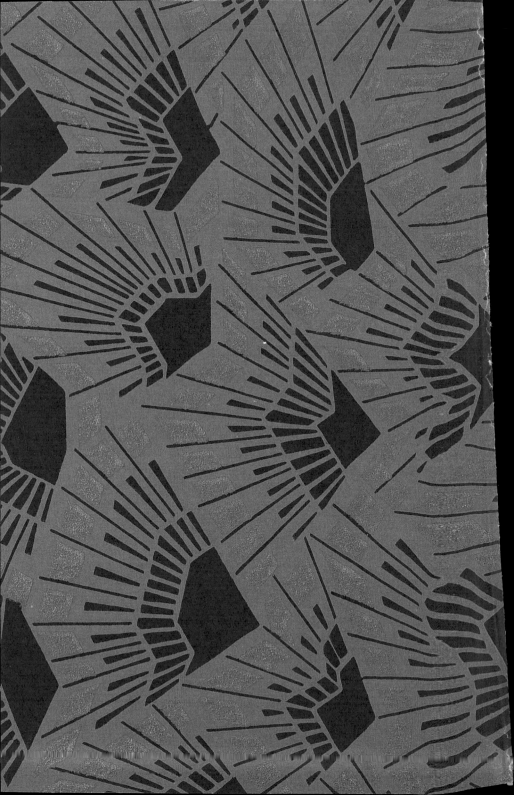